The Neue Pinakothek   Munich

Christian Lenz

The Neue Pinakothek   Munich

C H BECK / SCALA BOOKS

© Scala Publishers Ltd

First published in 1989 by
Scala Publishers Ltd
140a Shaftesbury Avenue
London WC2H 8HD

ISBN 1 870248 19 8

Photographs: photographic department of the Bayerische
Staatsgemäldesammlungen, Munich and Artothek, Planegg

© VG Bild-Kunst, Bonn, 1989: Max Beckmann, Pierre Bonnard,
Franz Defregger, Marice Denis, James Ensor, Aristide Maillol,
Claude Monet, Paul Sérusier, Paul Signac, Max Slevogt,
Edouard Vuillard

Designed by Alan Bartram
Translated from the German by Anthony Vivis and Tinch Minter
English text edited by Paul Holberton
Produced by Scala Publishers Ltd
Filmset by August Filmsetting, St Helens, England
Printed and bound by Editoriale Lloyd, Trieste, Italy

Contents

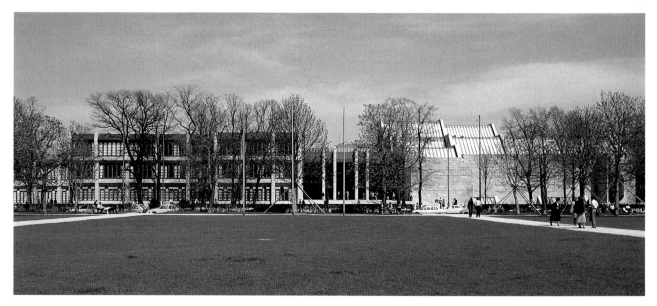

The Neue Pinakothek, new building
(1981), south side

The Neue Pinakothek Munich

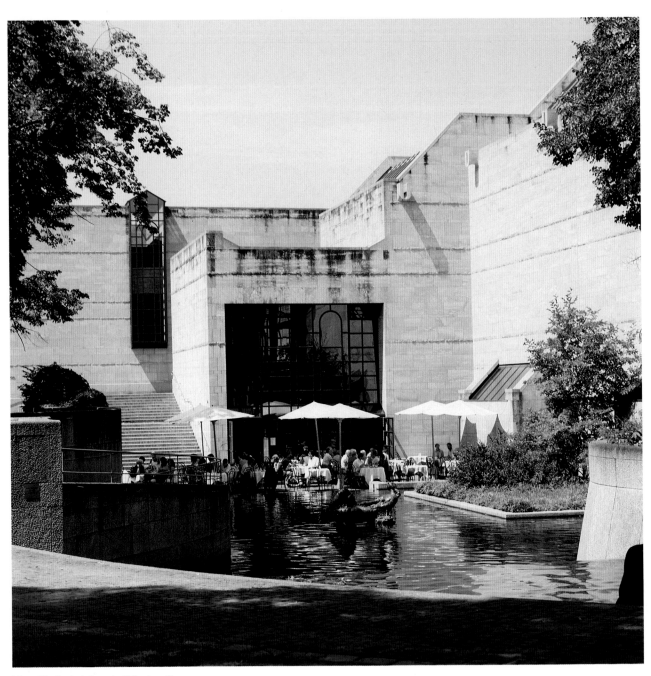

Neue Pinakothek (new building), café
terrace with fountain and pool

Introduction

The Neue Pinakothek is one of the several important museums which constitute the Bayerische Staatsgemäldesammlungen, or Bavarian State Collections. Its holdings amount to about 5,000 works of art, dating from the mid-eighteenth century to the early twentieth, with the emphasis on paintings and sculpture of the nineteenth century. About 550 works are on display.

Like the Alte Pinakothek (Old Master Gallery), the Neue Pinakothek (New Picture Gallery) was founded by King Ludwig I of Bavaria (born 1786, reigned 1825-48, died 1868). Already when Crown Prince (1799-1825), Ludwig had taken an active interest in contemporary art, especially German art, and even before his accession had managed to exert influence on its direction, pushing through the construction of the Glyptothek (Sculpture Gallery) from 1816 until its completion in 1830, and the appointments of Leo von Klenze as court architect in 1820 and of Peter Cornelius as director of the Munich Academy of Arts in 1824. As soon as he became king, he enthusiastically initiated a wide range of projects, personally involving himself in architecture, town-planning and the purchase and commission of works of art. The most important results for Munich of his activity were the creation of the Königsplatz (1816-48), the extension of the Residenz (1826-35) and the construction *ex novo* of the Alte Pinakothek (1826-36), the Allerheiligen-Hofkirche (Royal Church of All Saints, 1826-37), the Universitätskirche Sankt Ludwig (University Church of St Louis, 1829-43) and, rather later, the Neue Pinakothek (1846-53).

From his days as Crown Prince Ludwig had had frequent contact with artists, indeed he felt himself to be an artist. He acquired his first contemporary picture, a *Penitent Magdalen* by Heinrich Füger, in 1808. He especially favoured, among German artists, the members of the German community in Rome. 'The Fine Art of painting, which lay extinguished, has been rekindled in the nineteenth century by Germans ...', declared Ludwig at the laying of the foundation-stone of the Neue Pinakothek. His patronage was characterised by a passion for Italy and by strong patriotism, which the recent struggle against Napoleon may partly explain.

The Neue Pinakothek was not, however, Munich's first institution for the encouragement of contemporary art. The Kunstakademie (Academy of Arts) had been founded in 1808, not only to provide tuition and to exhibit its members' work but also more broadly 'as a centre of all artistic endeavour', which would have 'an artistically stimulating effect on the cultural life of the nation', according to Schelling's foundation charter. The foundation of the Kunstverein (Art Union) had followed in 1823, with a membership primarily of landscape and genre painters who wished to challenge the authority of the Academy. In 1838 Ludwig himself had promoted the construction of the Kunst- und Industrie-Ausstellungsgebäude (Halls for the Display of Arts, Crafts and Machines), intending to co-ordinate Akademie and Kunstverein exhibitions as international events which would rival those of Paris and Brussels. Ludwig began to plan for the construction of the Neue Pinakothek, and to collect art systematically to that end, in the 1830s.

When the Neue Pinakothek was opened in 1853, some 300 paintings could be exhibited, among which were important items from Leo von Klenze's collection, which Ludwig had acquired in 1841. The majority of works were genre or landscape, bought on the open market or at exhibitions of the Kunstverein. For the most part the history painters of the Academy received patronage in commissions for public buildings – Peter von Cornelius and his team in the Glyptothek, the Alte Pinakothek and the Ludwigskirche, Schnorr von Carolsfeld in the Residenz, Heinrich Hess and the Schraudolph brothers in the Allerheiligen-Hofkirche; Ludwig also commissioned Wilhelm von Kaulbach to make designs for the decoration of the Neue Pinakothek building.

The former Neue Pinakothek building
(colour lithograph of about 1860)

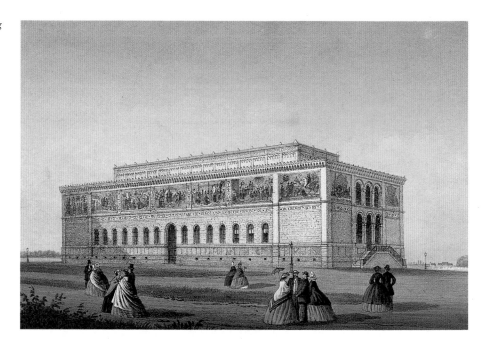

Designs for the Neue Pinakothek were initiated in 1842. Abandoning his original idea to erect a building on the Gasteig, the King acquired a plot north of the Alte Pinakothek in 1845 and laid the foundation-stone on 12th October 1846. Friedrich von Gärtner's plans were amended and the new building was carried out by August Voit, one of Gärtner's pupils. The Museum was opened on 25th October 1853. It was a square-cut, largely windowless edifice, 107 metres long and 29 metres wide, rising to 27 metres high: it was conceived as a basilica, with a 'nave' rising 5 metres above the 'aisles'. It was decorated on the outside with vast frescoes, running the whole perimeter of the upper storey, and depicting, in accordance with Ludwig's commission, '... recent developments in the Arts, called into being by *His Majesty the King*, and emanating from Munich'. The frescoes were executed by Christoph Nilson from Wilhelm von Kaulbach's designs.

The Neue Pinakothek was the first public museum in Europe devoted exclusively to contemporary art. Following Ludwig's death in 1868, the authorities began making new purchases in the 1880s. In 1891 Conrad Fiedler donated a large and important group of works by Hans von Marées; then, between 1911 and 1913, came the Tschudi Donation, with works by Manet, Rodin, Cézanne, Van Gogh and Gauguin, among others, given by several benefactors as a memorial to the late Hugo von Tschudi, former Director of the Galleries. In 1915 the Neue Pinakothek came under State control and was reorganized. As a result, in 1919, the more recent pictures were transferred to the Neue Staatsgalerie (now the Staatsgalerie Moderner Kunst, the State Gallery of Modern Art), but in 1981 were returned to the rebuilt Neue Pinakothek. Since 1945 acquisitions by the State have continued to be augmented by the generosity of private donors, who sometimes also make works available to the Gallery on long-term loan.

So great was the damage to King Ludwig's building in 1945 that it was decided to demolish it and construct another on the site. The foundation-stone of the second building, designed by Alexander von Branca, was laid on 16th July 1975, and the Museum was opened on 28th March 1981. It was designed to resemble the Alte Pinakothek in size, alignment, materials and finish, but not to outdo it or overpower it, and it was to maintain established German tradition in the design of museums, particularly that tradition as it had evolved in Munich. Traditional elements include the kind of façade and entrance hall it has, and the disposition of the exhibition rooms. The building was intended to welcome, hence the entrance front with its café terrace and fountain, and the lawns which surround the building, where sculptures by Henry Moore, Toni Stadler and Fritz Koenig, among others, are exhibited. The façade opposite the Alte Pinakothek has two different aspects, according to the different functions enclosed behind it: on the right, a massive wall secludes the exhibition areas, on the left the Museum's offices open to the world through rows of windows. The foyer that divides the two sides is entirely glazed, but contains within a monumental staircase, so that visitors have a sensation both of lightness and of strength. There is also a tripartite vertical division, between basement, wall and roofline. Severe symmetry, which would have been deadening, was avoided for the sake of a more complex relationship between the elements of the building. The spacious hall into which one enters, which, with its various facilities, is a kind of nodal point of the building, encourages the visitor to explore further.

The galleries are arranged in a figure-of-eight around two small, unroofed inner courts. Smaller annexes open off the main rooms, which are divided one from another by a series of corridors and gently rising steps (with ramps for wheel-chairs), so that the visitor clearly perceives the transition from one section to another. Different tones of pastel shades compound the effect. Small sympathetic lounges are also provided along the circuit. The galleries are designed not for troops of visitors passing through, but for interested individuals and small groups. Unlike modern synthetics, its natural or traditional materials – sandstone, granite, marble, various kinds of wood, brass and copper (which in time will patinate green) – will age pleasingly, especially in such favourable light. In a combination previously tried in the Alte Pinakothek, the vaulted rooms in the Neue Pinakothek are overhead-lit both naturally and artificially, bringing out the colours of the paintings to best possible effect. Harmonizing with the soft tones of the decoration, the strong but gentle light is also uplifting.

It remains to be added that the sections into which the Museum is so readably divided serve a didactic, or rather informative function. Anyone walking through the Museum will obtain a representative and sometimes very precise impression of developments in art from the middle of the eighteenth century to the beginning of the twentieth. However, the visitor will notice not only the differences between 'schools' and individual artists, but also a divide between works sometimes of great historical interest or importance, because typical of their period or highly successful in their own day, and others that conform rather better to today's expectations of what a great work of art should be. The visitor may like to reflect on the fact that the authors of the latter, artists such as Cézanne and Van Gogh, Marées and Leibl, achieved little or no recognition in their own lifetime.

1
Aristide Maillol
Banyuls-sur-Mer 1861 –
1944 Banyuls-sur-Mer
Flora, 1910-12, signed
Bronze, 163.5 cm high (including base)
Inv. no. B.154. Acquired in 1931 from
the Wolff collection, Munich.
This figure and three other statues
constitute a cycle of the Four Seasons,
which Maillol executed on commission
from the Russian collector Morosoff.

2
Carl Rottmann
Handschuhsheim 1797 –
1850 Munich
Marathon, 1848
Encaustic on stonecast, 157 × 200 cm
Inv. no. WAF 860. Acquired in 1845.
This picture is one of a cycle of landscapes of Greece, produced between
1838 and 1850 for King Ludwig I.
The cycle eventually comprised 32
pictures and was originally intended
for the arcades of the Hofgarten.
Reduced to 23 landscapes, it finally
found a home in a gallery of its own in
the Neue Pinakothek. Encaustic, the
medium in which Rottmann executed
the pictures, had recently been
developed in Munich.

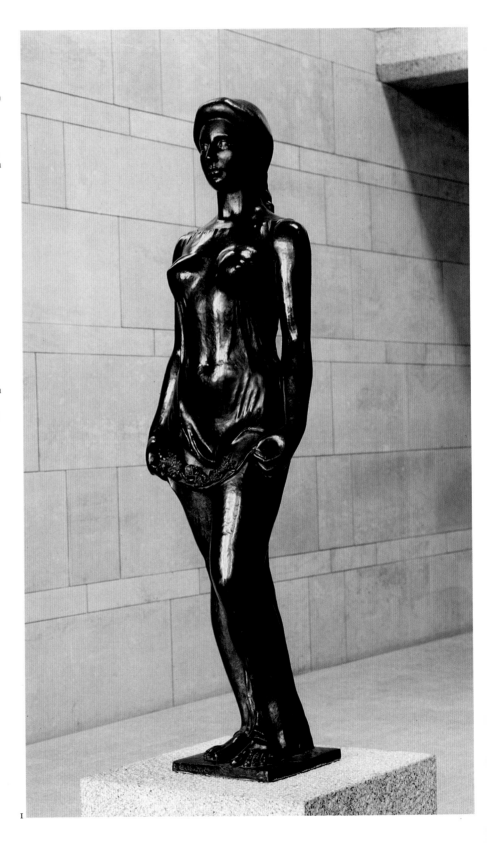

1

Entrance Hall

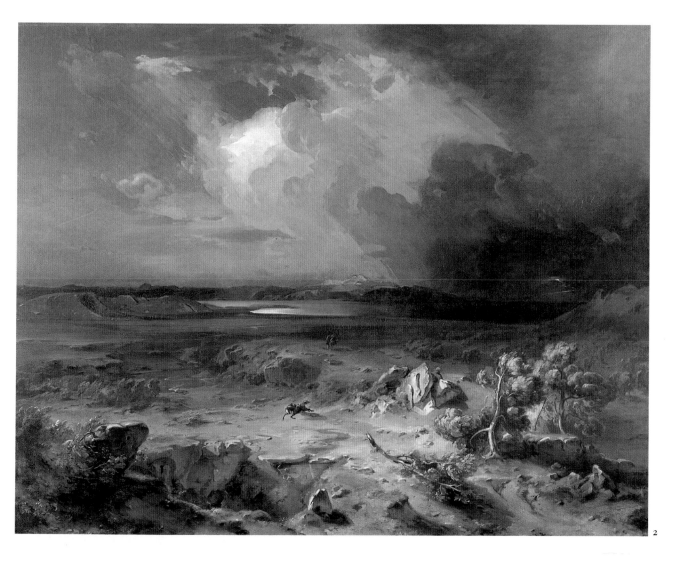

2

The entrance hall contains comparatively few works of art. However, sculptures by Auguste Rodin and Aristide Maillol, and four paintings from Carl Rottmann's *Greece* series, illustrate the range of the collection – Rottmann's paintings were commissioned by Ludwig I in the first half of the nineteenth century in Munich and for Munich, while the late nineteenth-century and early twentieth-century French sculptures prelude a gamut of works of international significance in the Gallery. Rodin's important early masterpiece, *The Age of Bronze* (1876), unfortunately is a fragment, for the statue was badly damaged in the terrible fire which in 1931 ravaged the Munich Glaspalast and entirely destroyed several German Romantic works. Models of the original and the present Neue Pinakothek are displayed on the first floor.

International art around 1800

Art of the years around 1800 reveals the great disruption which occurred in the time of the French Revolution and which affected all spheres of culture, including the arts. The French Revolution was not of course the cause of these far-reaching changes, rather their expression. Already before 1789 there had been a reaction against the artificialities of Rococo, and 'nature' had emerged as the new ideal. In the pursuit of this ideal artists had begun to seek an immediate response to the landscape, and in the human sphere upheld honesty, charity and such 'natural' virtues, both of the individual and of society, in pictures that were often explicitly moralistic.

In this section there is a large number of English paintings, although English paintings have been acquired systematically by the Museum only during the last few decades. There has been a growing awareness that this 'school' was not simply under-represented (not only in this Gallery but on the Continent in general), but also had vital relevance to the development of European painting as a whole. Many of these works are in many ways traditional – portraits reflecting the heritage of Van Dyck, landscapes in the mode of Claude, or even paintings responding to the more recent French trends set by Watteau, Mercier and Gravelot. In other ways they reveal a new relationship to nature, above all in the new immediacy with which the landscapes are painted or subjects are set in the landscape. A considerable factor in this development was the English landscape garden as it evolved from about 1730, certainly influencing landscape painting.

Almost all the important English painters of the eighteenth and nineteenth centuries are represented: there is a portrait by William Hogarth, otherwise known as a painter and engraver of moral tales, and pictures by George Stubbs, master painter of horses, by Sir Joshua Reynolds, first President of the Royal Academy and the author of significant *Discourses* on art, and by his rival Thomas Gainsborough, who besides his numerous portraits also painted many landscapes, in which he combined the influence of Claude with that of seventeenth-century Dutch art. There are also important examples of portraiture, so dominant in British art of the period, by George Romney, Henry Raeburn and Thomas Lawrence, who were active primarily in the second half of the eighteenth century, but lived on into the nineteenth. The landscapists John Constable and Joseph William Mallord Turner were also born in the eighteenth century, but their careers belong mostly to the nineteenth. Constable has exceptional importance in the history of landscape painting, since his influence was not only native but European, and his plain, straightforward vision of nature and unmixed colours made a great impression on Delacroix and the Barbizon School, and so on many others influenced by their ideas. Constable and also Turner had an important precursor in Richard Wilson, whose *View over the Thames*, full of feeling though it is simply a 'view', is one of the most impressive landscapes in the collection.

French art of the period is represented by an outstanding picture by Jacques-Louis David, his portrait of the Marquise de Sorcy de Thélusson. David, the leading French painter of his day, harnessed the new interpretations of the Antique which had earlier been suggested by the rise of archaeology and by the writer Winckelmann and the painter Mengs to the ideal then current of individual self-determination, though this involved at the same time recognition of moral and social obligations. David's bold, radically simple work, in all its immediacy, is a remarkable example of the modern trend in art. In the annex, both Anton Raphael Mengs's self-portrait and Heinrich Füger's portrait of Joseph Stieler to some extent share David's approach.

The most important and varied painter of the period was Francisco de Goya, court painter to the Spanish King Charles IV from 1789. His paintings include both religious and

Antonio Canova
Possagno 1757 – 1822 Venice
Paris, 1807-16
Marble, 205 cm high
Inv. no. WAF B.4. Acquired from the
artist by Crown Prince Ludwig in
1816.
Paris, a son of Priam, King of Troy,
was called upon to decide which of the
three goddesses, Hera, Athena and
Aphrodite, was the most beautiful. He
chose Aphrodite, and in return
received Helen as his wife – which
caused the Trojan War.

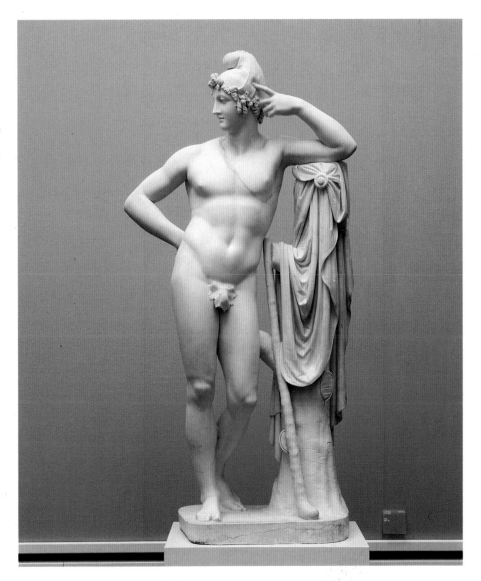

genre scenes (mostly cartoons for tapestries), though the majority are portraits, and he is
equally famous for his moralizing graphic work (*Caprichos*, 1797-98, *Desastres de la Guerra*
1810-20), in which he excoriated human weakness and suffering. Despite his formation in a
milieu of Italian and Spanish art between Baroque and Neoclassicism, he was a realist
painter who drew inspiration from Velázquez and Rembrandt. His pictures, whether
profound characterisations, sarcastic journalism or possessed visions, have an intensity no
contemporary matched. The Neue Pinakothek owns ten of his paintings, including a rare
still life.

   Besides the many paintings in this section Antonio Canova's statue of *Paris* may be
mentioned. It shows the Italian Neoclassicist's usual sensitivity.

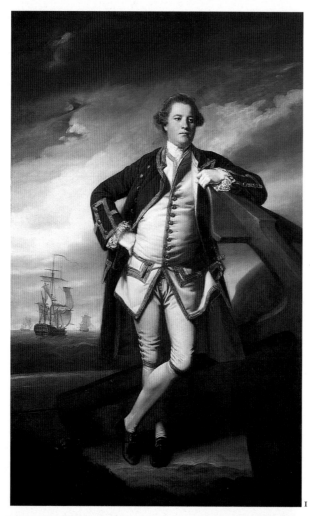

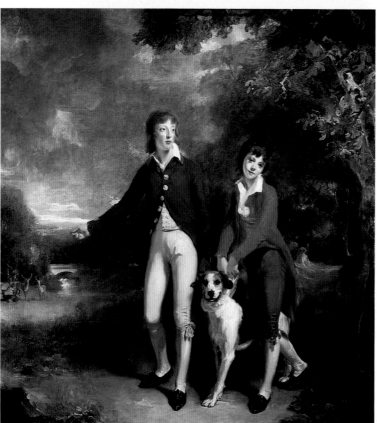

1
Sir Joshua Reynolds
Plympton Earl's 1723 –
1792 London
Captain Philemon Pownall, 1769
Canvas, 233 × 148 cm.
Inv. no. 14932. Acquired in 1985 from
L. Herner, Zurich.
Philemon Pownall was born and grew
up in Plymouth. He entered the Royal
Navy as a young man, and served as a
lieutenant under Admiral Boscawen.
As commander of the frigate *Apollo*,
on 5 June 1780, he was killed in a
naval engagement with the Spanish
frigate *Stanislaus*.

2
Sir Thomas Lawrence
Bristol 1769 – 1830 London
*The sons of the first Lord Talbot, c*1792
Canvas, 228.7 × 212.8 cm
Inv. no. 14882. Acquired in 1984 with
the aid of the Ernst von Siemens art
fund.
The subjects are Charles Chetwynd-
Talbot, Viscount Ingestre, and his
younger brother, the Hon John
Chetwynd-Talbot, in the grounds of
the family seat, Hensol Castle, over-
looking Cardiff Bay.

3
Richard Wilson
Penegoes 1714 – 1782 Colommendy
*View over the Thames at Kew Gardens
towards Syon House*, 1760-70, signed
Canvas, 104 × 138.5 cm
Inv. no. 14559. Acquired in 1978

4
Thomas Gainsborough
Sudbury 1727 – 1788 London
Mrs Thomas Hibbert, 1786
Canvas, 127 × 101.5 cm
Inv. no. FV 4. Acquired in 1978 by the
Verein zur Förderung der Alten und
Neuen Pinakothek.
In 1784, Sophia Boldero (1760-1829)
had married Thomas Hibbert, who
came from a long-established mercan-
tile family in Manchester.

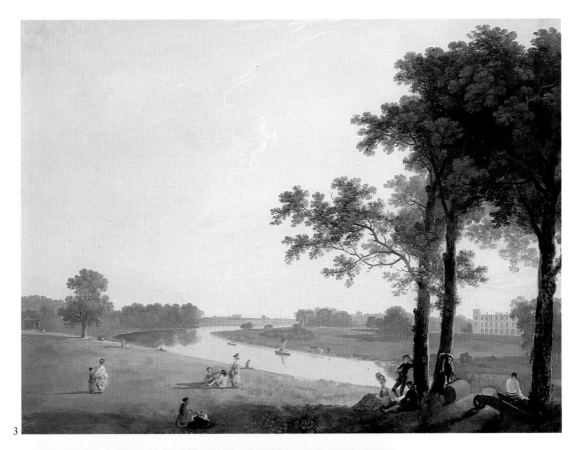

3

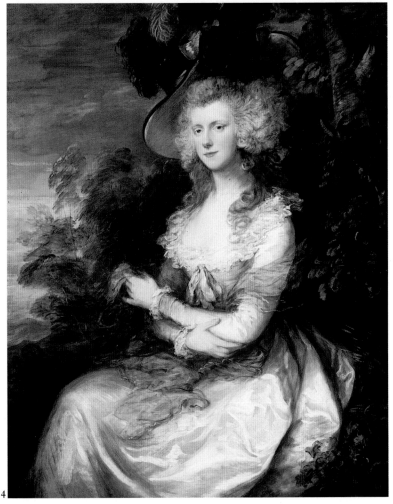

4

1

Johann Heinrich Fuseli
Zurich 1741 – 1825 London
Satan and Death, divided by Sin,
1792-1802
Canvas, 91.3 × 71.1 cm
Inv. no. 9494. Acquired in 1928 on the
Munich art market.
This is a scene from John Milton's
Paradise Lost (II, 702 ff), a work which
Fuseli illustrated in other pictures and
which also occupied other artists,
including William Blake.

2

George Romney
Dalton 1734 – 1802 Kendal
Catherine Clements, 1788, signed
Canvas, 127.4 × 102.3 cm
Inv. no. HUW 29. Acquired in 1974 for
the collection of the Bayerische
Hypotheken- und Wechselbank.
Catherine, the daughter of the Irish
statesman John Beresford, was born in
1760. In 1788 she married the Right
Honourable Henry Theophilus
Clements. She died in 1836.

3

Jacques-Louis David
Paris 1748 – 1825 Brussels
Marquise de Sorcy de Thélusson, 1790,
signed and dated
Canvas, 129 × 97 cm
Inv. no. HUW 21. Acquired in 1971 for
the collection of the Bayerische
Hypotheken- und Wechselbank.
Anne-Marie-Louise Rilliet (1770-
1845), the eldest daughter of a Geneva
banker, was painted by David shortly
after her marriage to the Marquis de
Sorcy de Thélusson. The commission
came from her uncle, for whom David
also painted the portrait of Anne-
Marie-Louise's aunt, his sister,
Jeanne-Robertine, later Marquise
d'Orvillier (now in the Louvre).

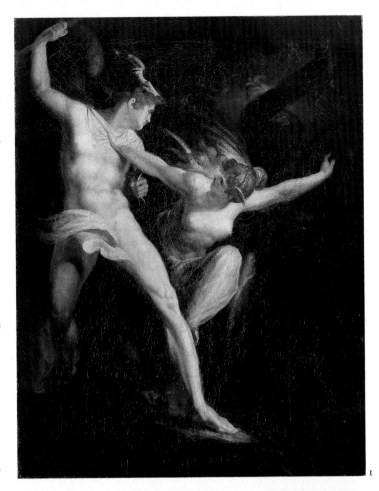

1

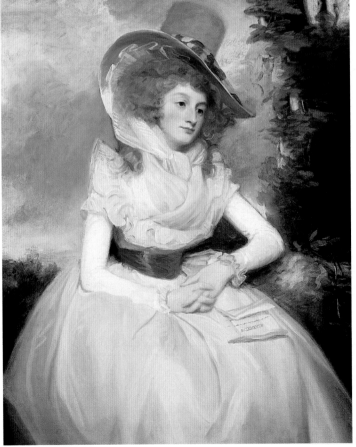

2

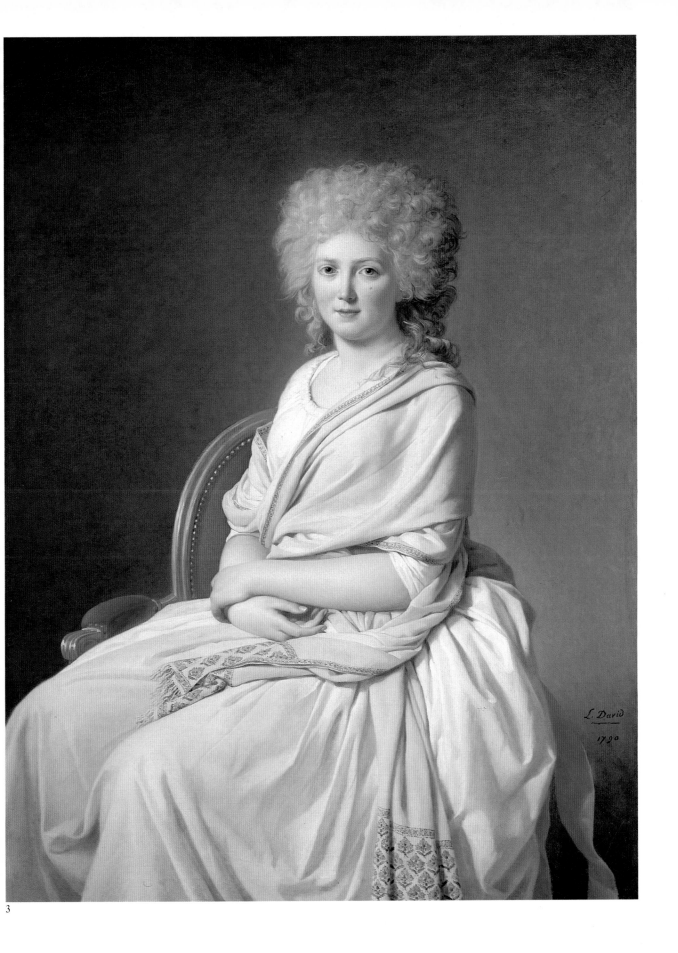

3

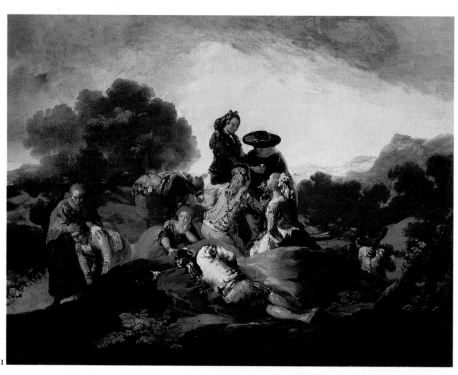

1

Francisco José Goya y Lucientes
Fuendetodos 1746 – 1828 Bordeaux
A party in the countryside, 1776
Canvas, 40.2 × 54.6 cm
Inv. no. HUW 23. Acquired in 1973 for the collection of the Bayerische Hypotheken- und Wechselbank.
This picture was painted on commission from the Marqués de Montvirgen y San Carlo as a memento of an excursion. It possibly also served as a study for a large cartoon, now lost, for a tapestry. In 1776, Goya is known to have supplied the royal tapestry factory with a cartoon of the same title, 'La Merienda Campestre'.

2

Francisco José Goya y Lucientes
Fuendetodos 1746 – 1828 Bordeaux
Doña Maria Teresa da Vallabriga,
c1783
Canvas, 151.2 × 97.8 cm
Inv. no. HUW 2. Acquired in 1966 for the collection of the Bayerische Hypotheken- und Wechselbank.
In 1776, Maria Teresa (1758-1828) married the Infante, Don Luis de Borbón, sixth son of Philip V and younger brother of Charles III. Archbishop of Seville and Toledo, and finally a Cardinal, he relinquished orders so as to be able to marry Doña Maria Teresa.

3

Francisco José Goya y Lucientes
Fuendetodos 1746 – 1828 Bordeaux
Don José Queraltó in the uniform of a Spanish military doctor, 1802, signed and dated
Canvas, 101.5 × 76.1 cm
Inv. no. 9334. Acquired in 1925 on the Berlin art market.
Don José Queraltó, who was born in Tarragona, and died in Madrid in 1805, was a surgeon and writer, a professor at the Real Colegio de Medicina y Cirurgia de San Carlos, Madrid, and from 1793 onwards director of the hospitals in Navarra and Guipúzcoa. He is wearing the uniform of a military doctor with the rank of general. Goya is reputed to have given him the portrait in gratitude for medical help.

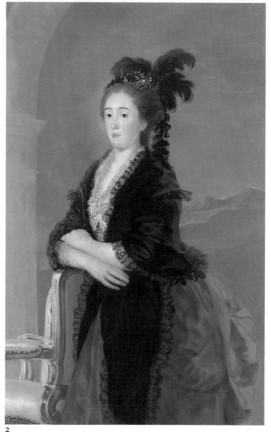

2

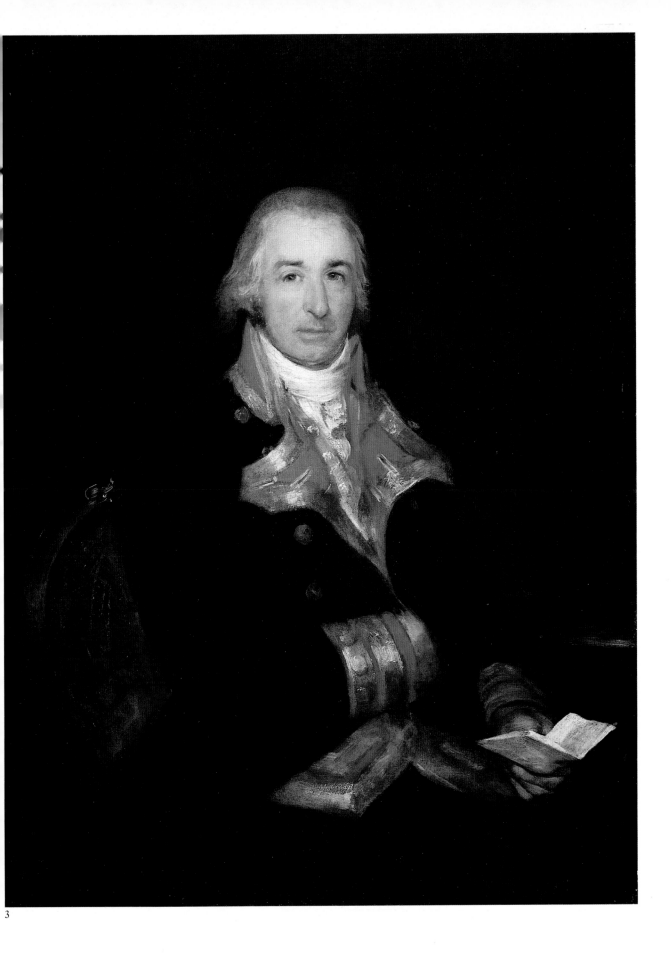

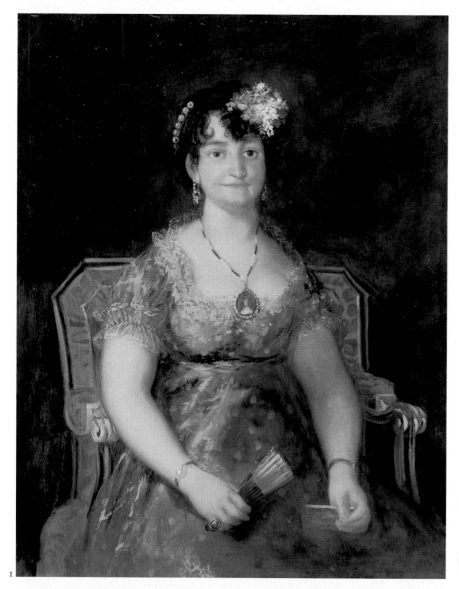

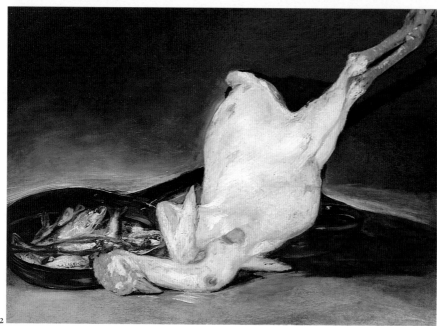

1

Franciso José Goya y Lucientes
Fuendetodos 1746 – 1828 Bordeaux
Marquesa de Caballero, 1807, signed
and dated
Canvas, 104.7 × 83.7 cm
Inv. no. HUW 13. Acquired in 1968 for
the collection of the Bayerische
Hypotheken- und Wechselbank.
The sitter's full title was Doña Maria
Soledad de la Rocha Fernandez de la
Peña, Marquesa de Caballero (1774-
1809). In 1795, she became lady-in-
waiting to Queen Maria Luisa of
Spain, and in 1800 married the
Marqués de Caballero (1770-1821),
who was Spanish Minister of Justice
from 1798 to 1808. Goya painted a
portrait of her husband as a pendant.

2

Francisco José Goya y Lucientes
Fuendetodos 1746 – 1828 Bordeaux
Plucked turkey, c1815, signed
Canvas, 44.8 × 62.4 cm
Inv. no. 8575
Acquired in 1909 on the Paris art
market.
This picture is one of the relatively
small number of Goya's still lifes, and
is an example of the genre called
'bodegones' or kitchen scenes, for
which there is a Spanish tradition
going back to the early seventeenth
century.

3

John Constable
East Bergholt 1776 – 1837 London
Dedham Vale seen from East Bergholt,
c1825
Canvas, 45.6 × 55.1 cm
Inv. no. FV 5. Acquired in 1982 by
the Verein zur Förderung der Alten
und Neuen Pinakothek.
Constable had a studio built in the
grounds of the mill his parents owned
in East Bergholt. To paint this view,
the artist evidently took up a standpoint some 300 metres south-west of
the studio.

4

Sir David Wilkie
Cults 1785 – 1841 at sea
The Reading of the Will, 1820, signed
and dated
Panel, 76 × 115 cm
Inv. no. WAF 1194. Acquired by King
Maximilian I of Bavaria, for whom it
was painted.
The scene is taken from Walter Scott's
novel *Guy Mannering*, where it follows
the funeral of Lady Singleside. But
Bannister had already put it on the
stage before Wilkie took it as a subject
for his painting. When he exhibited at
the Royal Academy it was an immediate and extraordinary success; Wilkie
soon became the most celebrated
painter of genre in England.

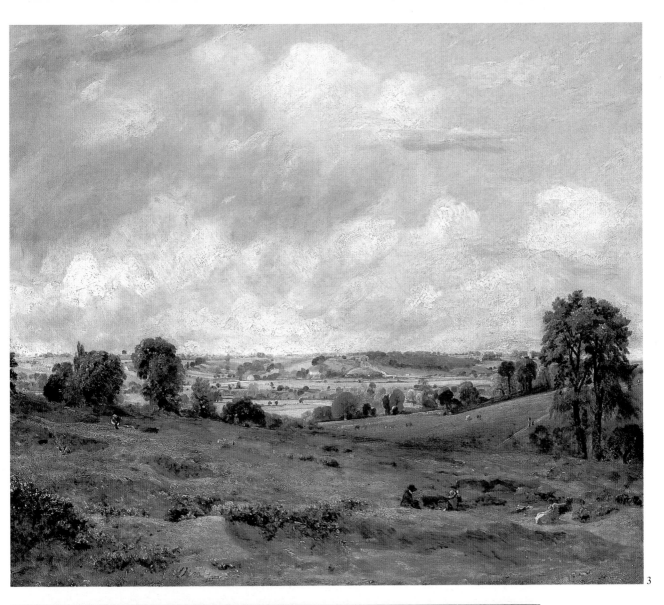

3

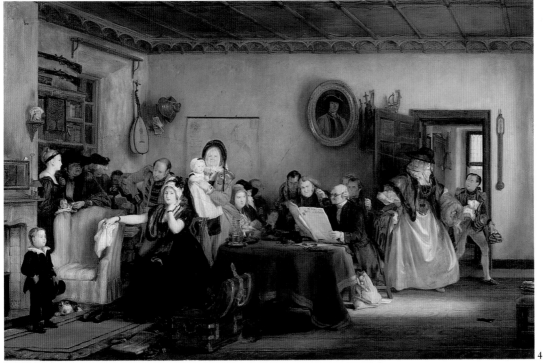

4

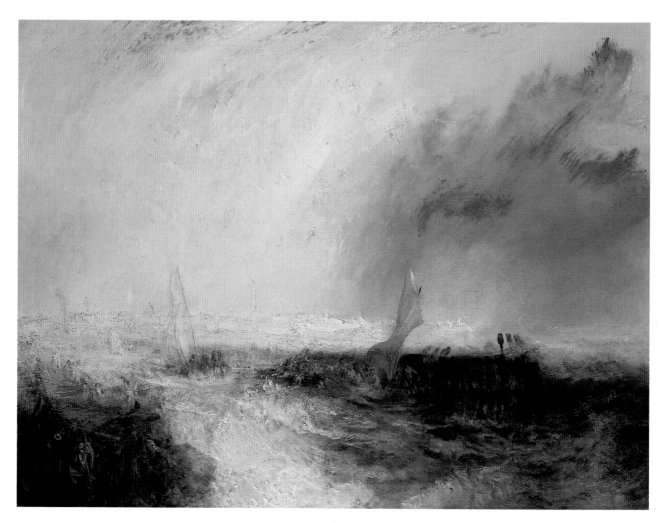

Joseph Mallord William Turner
London 1775 – 1851 London
Ostend, 1844
Canvas, 91.8 × 122.3 cm
Inv. no. 14435. Acquired in 1976 on
the London art market

Early Romantic art

This section features mainly German painting of the early nineteenth century, with important examples from the main centres of Dresden, Berlin and Munich. Strictly the term 'Romantic' applies only to some of the works, and even for these it is more a tag than a proper description.

Dresden had become one of the artistic capitals of Europe in the eighteenth century, and, though most famous for its Baroque achievements, also contributed to the rise of Neoclassicism. The archaeological writer Johann Joachim Winckelmann and Anton Raphael Mengs (whose self-portrait is in Room 2a) spent formative years there, and Winckelmann published his *Reflections on the Imitation of the Greek Arts* in Dresden in 1755. Around 1800, there was an equally important circle at Dresden of Romantic writers – Schelling, the Schlegel brothers, Novalis, Tieck and Wackenroder – whose work in general drew inspiration from the city's collection of paintings and its beautiful countryside, and some of whom in particular discussed the visual arts (for instance Wilhelm Wackenroder's *Heartfelt Effusions of an Art-loving Monk*, 1797, or August Wilhelm and Caroline von Schlegel's essays appearing under the title *Paintings*, 1799). During the same period there were also painters active in Dresden. The most important was Caspar David Friedrich, who, having completed his studies at the Copenhagen Academy, settled in the city in 1798, and had as associates there, among others of lesser rank, Carl Gustav Carus, Georg Friedrich Kersting and the Norwegian-born Johan Christian Dahl. Friedrich's art is characterised by its religious feeling (which was widespread among the early Romantics) and its nationalism, which had been aroused by Germany's political and military conflict with France. His landscapes show a deep feeling for the richness of nature, and often seem not merely observed, but actually experienced. Friedrich's tendency to symbolism, the belief conveyed by his landscapes that 'a man's reach should exceed his grasp', and his conception of the cyclical nature of life set him apart from the more factual, sometimes unimaginative outlook of Dahl or even of Karl Blechen, a leading Berlin painter with whom Friedrich was on close terms. Kersting, unlike these men, was not so much a landscapist as a painter of everyday bourgeois life, whose small-scale works of great sensibility herald Biedermeier painting of the middle decades of the nineteenth century.

The Munich 'school' is represented above all by Dillis, Kobell, Klenze and Rottmann, artists united by a common purpose to a much lesser extent than those in Dresden. Wilhelm von Kobell was a painter of serene landscapes, usually in a clear morning light, though he specialised in battle-scenes and animal pictures. Carl Rottmann, born in Heidelberg, painted more dramatic landscape setpieces, which reached their fulfilment in his *Greece* cycle, inspired as much by Grecian history as by its terrain. The two works by Leo von Klenze in the Gallery reveal his skills an archaeologist and architect. As Hofbauintendant (court architect) from 1820, he was largely responsible for the urban planning of the city and for the construction of such buildings as the Alte Pinakothek and the Glyptothek. His extensive studies in archaeology and ancient Greek architecture bore fruit in the recommendations for the protection of Greek antiquities put into effect by King Ludwig's son Otto when he became King of Greece (1832-62). Klenze would not have liked to be known as a Romantic: on the contrary, in 1818, according to Ringseis, 'this inveterate Hellenist ... lost all control on hearing of the Crown Prince's unexpected conversion' to medieval art, which held such interest for the Romantics.

1
Georg Friedrich Kersting
Güstrow 1785–1847 Meissen
Young woman sewing by the light of a
lamp, 1828, signed
Canvas, 40.3 × 34.2 cm
Inv. no. 14603. Acquired in 1979 from
the Rudolf Neumeister Gallery,
Munich

2
Johann Christian Clausen Dahl
Bergen 1788–1857 Dresden
The day after a stormy night, 1819,
signed and dated
Canvas, 74.5 × 105.6 cm
Inv. no. 14631. Acquired in 1980 from
a Norwegian private collection.
The artist considered this picture,
which he completed in eight days, his
best work. Contrary to the opinion of
Academic critics, he believed that the
viewer must have experienced the hos-
tile side of Nature in order to appreciate his rather rough and ready
picture.

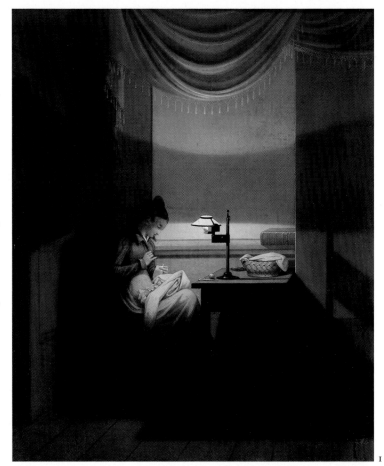
1

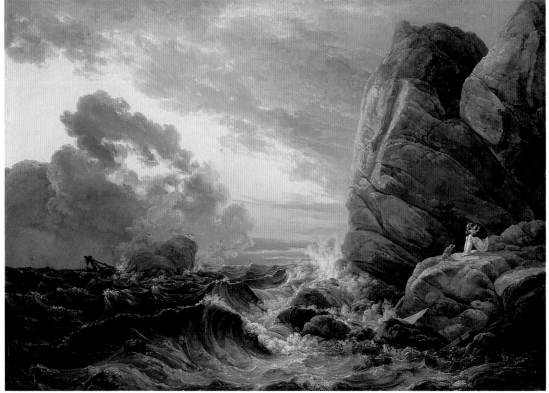
2

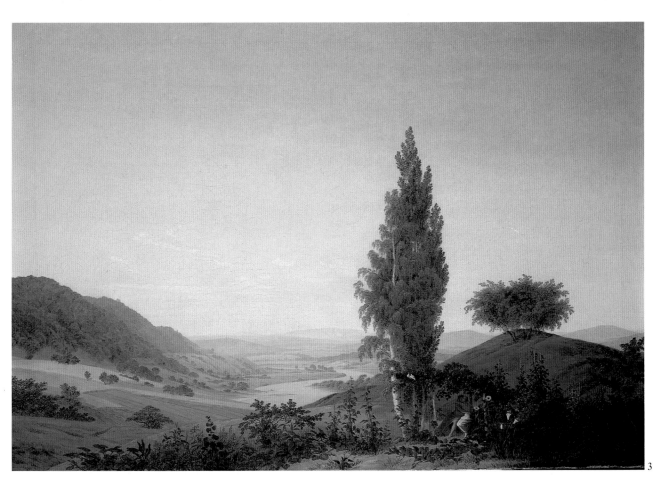

3

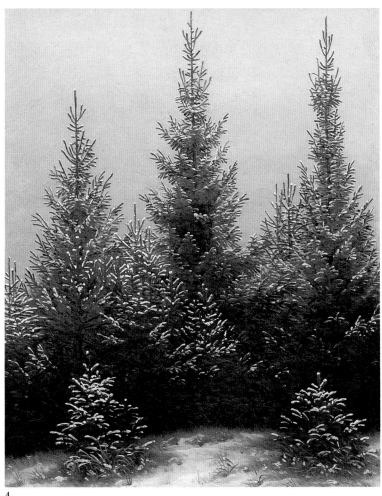

3
Caspar David Friedrich
Greifswald 1774 – 1840 Dresden
Summer, 1807
Canvas, 71.4 × 103.6 cm
Inv. no. 9702. Acquired in 1931 on the
Munich art market.
Friedrich painted a *Winter* as a companion piece to this picture. Seasonal
pictures of this kind were favourite
subjects of the artist.

4
Caspar David Friedrich
Greifswald 1774 – 1840 Dresden
*Pine thicket in snow, c*1828
Canvas, 30 × 24 cm
Inv. no. ESK 1. Acquired in 1983 for
the collection of the Ernst von
Siemens art fund.
Also in this case Friedrich painted a
companion piece, *Trees and bushes in
snow* (Dresden).

4

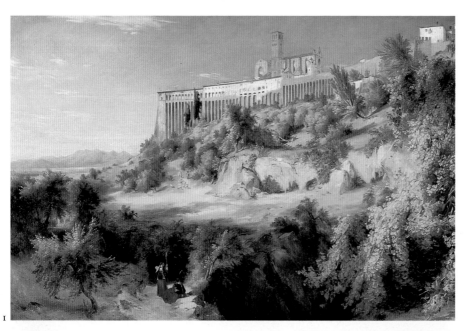

1

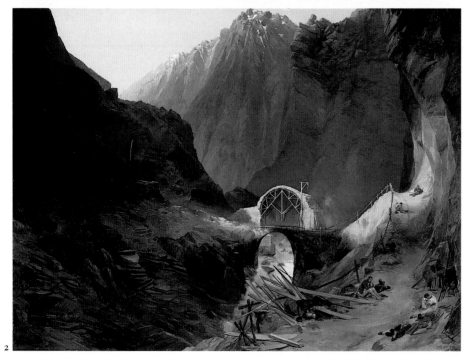

2

1

Karl Blechen
Cottbus 1798 – 1840 Berlin
*View of Assisi, c*1830
Canvas, 97 × 146.3 cm
Inv. no. 10338. Acquired in 1937 from
a private collection.
Blechen lingered in Assisi in 1829 for
several days on his way home from
Rome and painted several other
versions of this view of the church of
San Francesco. He worked up this
large picture in Berlin from his
sketches.

2

Karl Blechen
Cottbus 1798 – 1840 Berlin
The construction of the Devil's Bridge,
*c*1830
Canvas, 77.6 × 104.5 cm
Inv. no. L.1039. On loan from the
Bundesrepublik Deutschland.
On his way back from Italy in 1829,
Blechen also made several sketches of
the so-called Devil's Bridge at the St
Gotthard Pass. He evidently painted
up this picture shortly afterwards.

3

Wilhelm von Kobell
Mannheim 1766 – 1853 Munich
The Seige of Cosel, 1808, signed and
dated
Canvas, 202 × 305 cm
Inv. no. 3822. Passed from the private
collection of King Ludwig I to the
State in 1832.
This oil-painting is one of a twelve-
part cycle which the Crown Prince
Ludwig had commissioned from the
painter. The cycle depicted Bavaria's
victories for the Rhenish League
against Prussia and Russia. According
to an inscription on the reverse of the
picture, this represents the third
breakout made by the Prussian garri-
son from the fortress of Cosel in
Silesia. It was repulsed on 15 March
1806 by the Bavarians under Major
General von Raglovich.

4

Wilhelm von Kobell
Mannheim 1766 – 1835 Munich
View of the River Isar near Munich,
1819, signed and dated
Panel, 40.5 × 53.5 cm
Inv. no. 9213. Acquired in 1924 from a
private collection

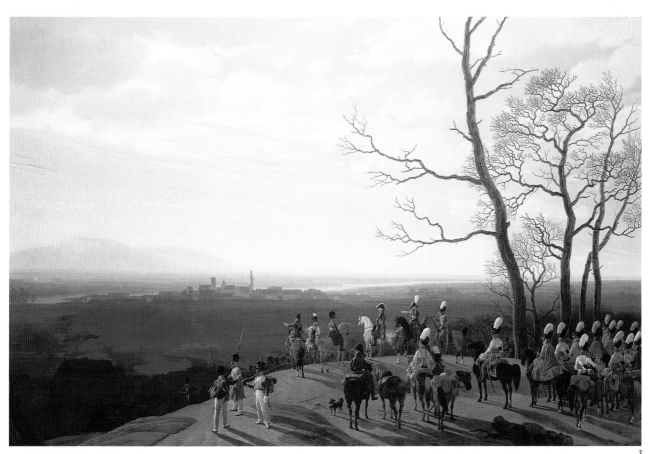

3

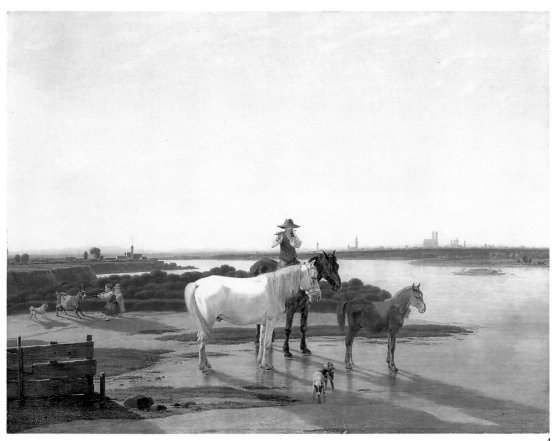

4

1
Leo von Klenze
Schleden 1784–1864 Munich
The Acropolis of Athens, 1846, signed
and dated
Canvas, 102.8 × 147.7 cm
Inv. no. 9463. Acquired by King
Ludwig I, and State property since
1927.

In 1820, the architect Leo von Klenze
was appointed Superintendant of
Buildings in Bavaria. In 1834, he was
sent on a diplomatic mission to
Athens, where Ludwig's son, Otto,
was King. Whilst in Greece, he took
an active interest in antiquities, taking
detailed measurements of them and
making provision for their special pro-

tection. He created this pictorial
reconstruction of the Acropolis from
an exact knowledge. This is one of the
considerable number of attractive
paintings by the architect.

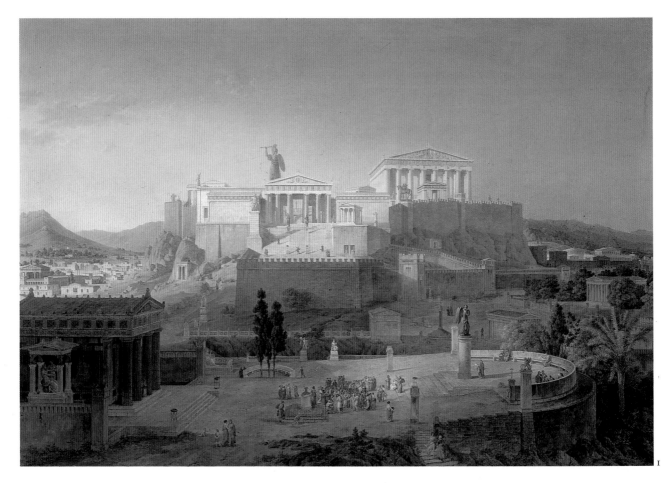

1

2
Johann Georg von Dillis
Grüngiebing 1759–1841 Munich
The Von Triva Palace, 1797, signed
and dated
Panel, 19 × 26.3 cm
Inv. no. 9392. Acquired in 1927 from a
private collection in Starnberg.
The small palace, which Privy Coun-
cillor Von Ostwaldt had built in 1705
at one end of what is now Brienner-
strasse (to the north of what was the
Kapuzinergraben), was later owned by
Privy Councillor Von Trivia. From
1785 onwards, it belonged to Karl
Albert von Aretin, whose son Adam
was taught to draw by Dillis. Dillis
already had a close relationship with
Ludwig I while he was still Crown
Prince. In 1822, he became Director of
the Central Art Gallery.

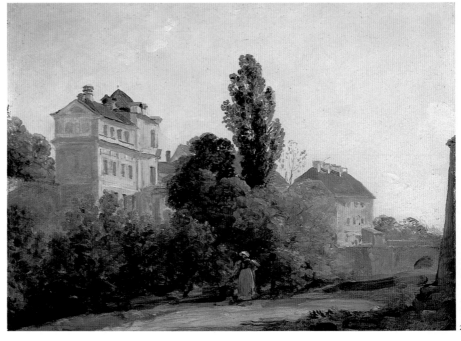

2

The court art of Ludwig I

Franz Ludwig Catel
Berlin 1778–1856 Rome
Crown Prince Ludwig in a Spanish inn at Rome, 1824, dated on the back on a slip of paper also identifying the persons
Canvas, 63 × 73 cm
Inv. no. WAF 142. From the private collection of Ludwig I.
This depicts the later King Ludwig I of Bavaria, surrounded by German artists in Rome. In a letter of 20 March 1824 to the art critic Gottlieb von Quandt, Catel wrote: '... I have just finished a small *bambocciata* for the Crown Prince of Bavaria. His Royal Highness had graciously arranged an intimate *déjeuner* at Don Raffaele's on the Ripa Grande, to mark Herr von Klenze's departure. He commanded me to immortalize the scene in paint ... From left to right the subjects are: mine host, Crown Prince Ludwig, Thorvaldsen, Leo von Klenze, Count Seinsheim, Johann Martin Wagner (standing), Phillip Veit, Dr Ringseis (standing), Julius Schnorr von Carolsfeld, Catel, and Baron Gumppenburg. Through the open door the Aventine Hill on the far side of the Tiber can be seen ...'

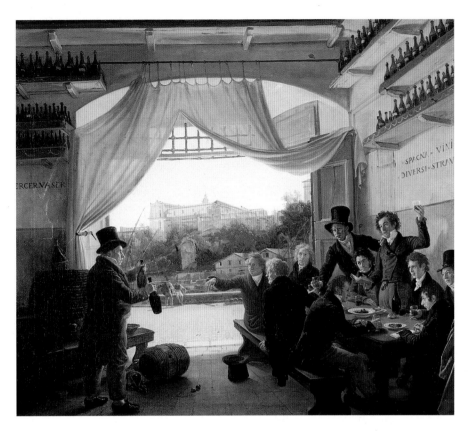

Munich owes the position it attained in the nineteenth century as a leading centre of the arts in Europe largely to the energy of Ludwig I. This section (and also the neighbouring rooms) contain works by the artists most favoured by the King, portraits of the most important personalities in his circle, and representations of the events in which he was directly or indirectly involved. It includes for instance cultural documents such as Franz Catel's group portrait of Ludwig with German artists in Rome, or works by Peter von Hess showing scenes from the career of Ludwig's son Otto in Bavaria and as King of Greece. The portraits include that of Wilhelm von Schelling and Joseph Stieler's of Goethe, one of the most penetrating likenesses of the poet ever made. Ludwig himself commissioned Stieler's portrait and many other pictures here, and others he bought directly from the artist or at exhibitions.

It is obvious from the works here and in adjoining sections, as from the whole range of his activity as a collector and promoter, that the King's taste was accommodating and catholic, even to the point of contradiction. Ludwig could appreciate both the Antique and the medieval, both Klenze's and Thorwaldsen's classicism and the Nazarenes' sentimentalism, and even the realist genre work of a painter like Dillis, dedicated more to nature. He was nevertheless dogmatically committed to art, declaring at the laying of the foundation-stone of the Neue Pinakothek, 'Art should not be regarded as a luxury. It has a part in every aspect of existence, it crosses over into life, and where there is no art there is no proper life. My great artists are my pride and my joy. The statesman's work will have long since passed away, while the creations of great artists continue to delight and to inspire.'

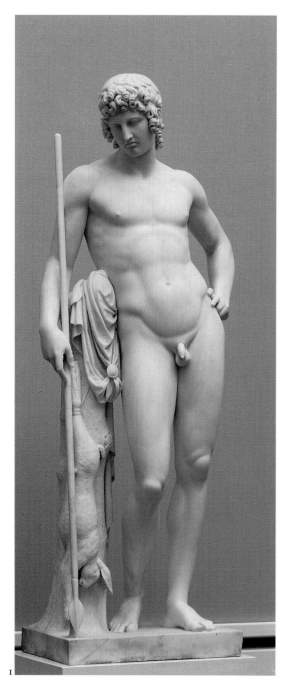

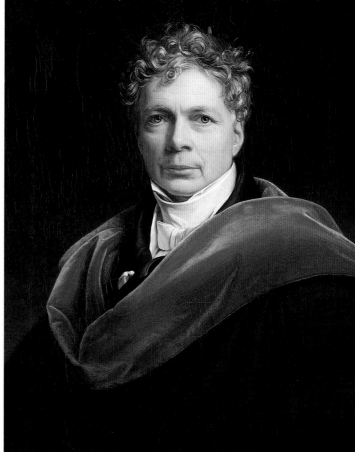

1

Bertel Thorvaldsen
Copenhagen 1770 –
1844 Copenhagen
Adonis, 1808-32, signed
Marble, 182 cm high
Inv. no. WAF-B.29. Acquired by King
Ludwig I.
Adonis the hunter was famous in
Greek mythology for his beauty. Aphrodite, goddess of Love, and Persephone, goddess of the Dead, fought
over him fiercely. It was settled that he
should spend two thirds of the year on
earth with Aphrodite, and the other
third with Persephone in the Under-
world. This symbolized the annual
death and rebirth of nature.
Crown Prince Ludwig commissioned
the statue from Thorvaldsen in 1808,
but the sculptor did not complete it
until 1832. This is one of the few
works – if not indeed the only one – he
completed entirely by his own hand.

2

Joseph Karl Stieler
Mainz 1781 – 1858 Munich
Friedrich Wilhelm von Schelling, 1835,
signed
Canvas, 71.5 × 58 cm
Inv. no. L.1858. On loan from the
Bayerische Verwaltung der
staatlichen Schlösser, Gärten und
Seen, Munich.

In 1798, Schelling (1775-1854) was
appointed by Goethe as Professor of
Philosophy at Jena, but in 1803 he
moved to Würzburg. In 1808, he took
up the position of General Secretary at
the Academy of Fine Arts, Munich.
He became Professor of Philosophy at
Munich University in 1827, then
Director of the Science Academy and
Curator of the scientific collections. In
1840, he was appointed to the University of Berlin, but he soon gave up
teaching in order to devote himself to
writing.

3

Joseph Karl Stieler
Mainz 1781 – 1858 Munich
Johann Wolfgang von Goethe, 1828
Canvas, 78.2 × 63.8 cm
Inv. no. WAF 1048. Acquired in 1828
by King Ludwig I.
This painting was commissioned by
Ludwig I and painted in Weimar. The
piece of paper in the poet's hand
shows the first lines of a poem Ludwig
had written in 1818:
Yes! Just as the flower Flora herself rene.
Through the seed which she widely strews
So one work of art succeeds another,
For life is mother to a new life;
Once feelings have become a work of art
Another splendid work through the strife
Of millennia will appeal to the heart.
Autumn, 1818.   Ludwig.

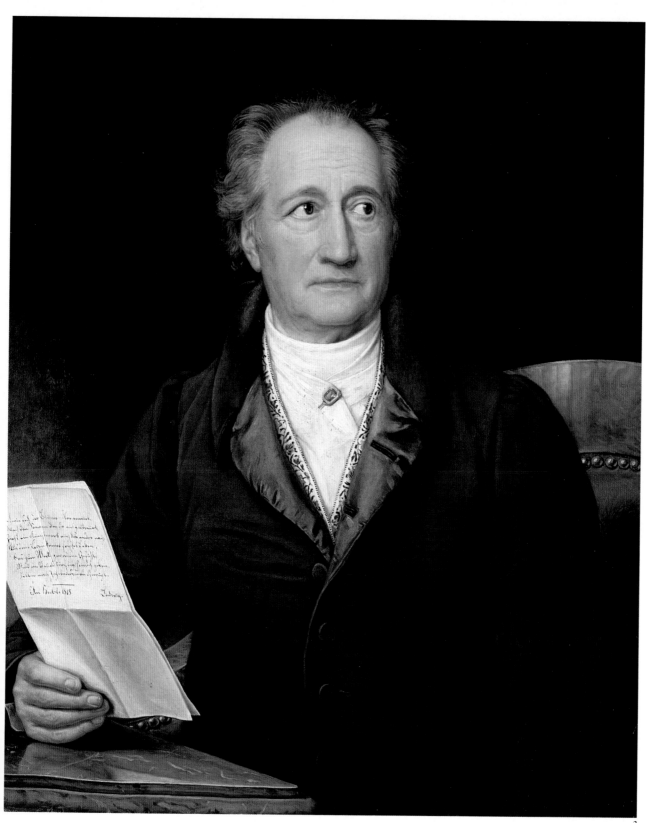

3

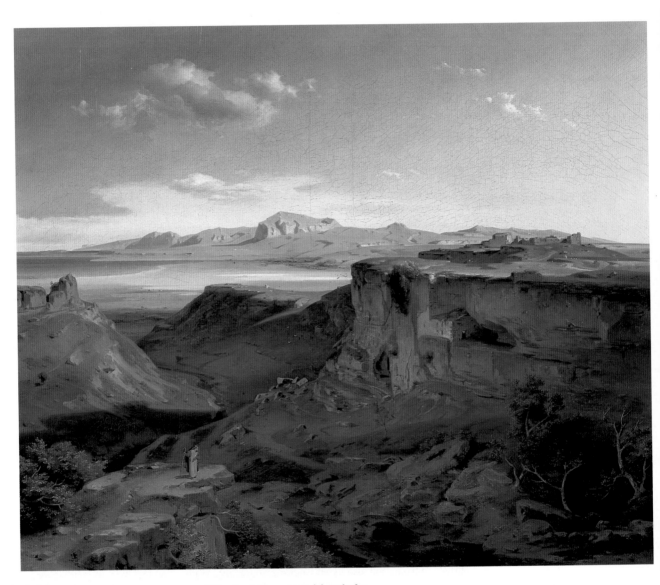

Carl Rottmann
Handschuhsheim 1797 –
1850 Munich
Sikyon and Corinth, 1836-38
Canvas, 85.2 × 102 cm
Inv. no. WAF 843. Acquired in 1841-42
from the collection of Leo von Klenze
by King Ludwig I.

This oil-painting was a trial study for
one of the encaustic pictures of
Rottmann's *Greece* cycle (see p.7).
Above right, on the plateau, are the
remains of the acropolis of Sikyon; and
in the background, towards the sea,
the ruins of Corinth.

German artists in Rome

Chronologically the first of the artists represented in this section is Jakob Philipp Hackert, who from 1768 lived in Rome, then in Naples and Florence. He knew Winckelmann and Mengs, and made the acquaintance of Goethe during Goethe's travels in Italy. Goethe thought highly of him and arranged for his autobiography to be published in 1811. Hackert painted exact and detailed landscape views; for Goethe, his 'portraits of landscapes were perfect likenesses', and he praised his 'views', 'prospects' and 'illustrations', but distinguished them from landscapes proper, which for him were the ideal visions of Claude and Poussin.

Poussin and similar artists were again the point of reference for Joseph Anton Koch, of the next generation after Hackert. Koch reached Rome in 1795, and there knew Johann Christian Reinhardt, Asmus Jacob Carstens and the Danish sculptor Thorwaldsen. Following the example of his teacher Adam Friedrich Oeser, Reinhardt painted heroic classical landscapes in the mode of Poussin and Claude, and was himself influential on his slightly younger contemporary Koch, who set out to represent his experiences of the Swiss Alps in the style of Poussin and Gaspard Dughet. Koch combined numerous different studies to create ambitious compositions such as *Schmadribachfall* (The waterfall at Schmadri) or *Heroic landscape with rainbow*. Although he tackled Nature on a grand scale, individual details are closely observed, and placed in relationship with the whole.

Koch is a significant figure in German art not only because of his classicizing tendencies. He also had connections with the Nazarenes, sharing their interest in Early Renaissance Italian painting and religious subjects. Between 1825 to 1829 he finished the cycle of paintings the Nazarene Peter von Cornelius had begun, and Philipp Veit had continued, in the Sala Dante of the Casino Massimo in Rome. He was influential on German art not only in Italy but also in Germany, after his *Heroic landscape* had been bought in 1815 by the Munich Academy of Arts as an exemplary exercise in the genre. Meanwhile Koch was able to make his work available and impart his ideas to a number of students in Rome, among them the Dresden painter Ludwig Richter.

Richter completed his mountain landscape in the Gallery, *The Watzmann*, in 1824, a year after meeting Koch, and the influence of Koch's recently completed *Scmadribachfall* is obvious. However, in contrast to Koch's mature handling, which conveys the grandeur and gravity of the Alpine landscape, Richter's work has a prettier, altogether more bland and tranquil aspect. In the three years in which he remained in Italy Richter was also drawn to Ernst Fries, his close contemporary, who, after studying in Heidelberg and Munich, came to Rome in the same year, 1823. Fries was influenced not only by the circle of German artists in Rome but also by an Englishman, George Wallis, who had lived in Heidelberg from 1812 to 1816 and taught landscape-painting there both to Fries and to Carl Rottmann. It was probably Fries who introduced Wallis to the practice of establishing the landscape space in gradations of tone, which distinguishes his work from that of Koch and Reinhardt.

Ludwig Richter
Dresden 1803 – 1884 Dresden
The Watzmann, 1824, signed and dated
Canvas, 120.2 × 93 cm
Inv. no. 8983. Acquired in 1918 from a
private collection in Dresden.
The Watzmann is a range in the western, Salzburg or Upper Austrian Alps
in Bavaria, south-west of Berchtes-
gaden. Its highest peak attains 2713
metres. This was the first major picture Richter painted after his arrival in
Rome, in autumn 1823. He worked it
up from travel sketches in the studio of
Joseph Anton Koch. Koch's recently
completed landscape *Schmadribachfall*
may well have inspired him.

2
Ernst Fries
Heidelberg 1801 – 1833 Karlsruhe
Amalfi, 1829, signed and dated
Canvas, 58.3 × 76.9 cm
Inv. no. 12528. Transferred from State
ownership in 1957.
In 1826 Fries made two visits to
Amalfi. In this picture, he depicted the
view over Amalfi from a standpoint
above the monastery of San Francesco.
As was usual, he completed the picture
only after his return home.

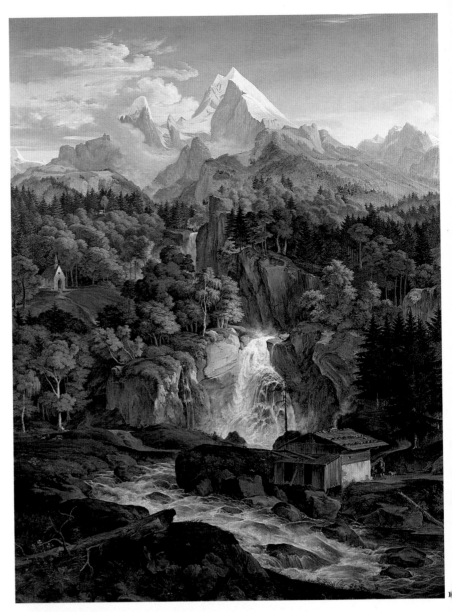

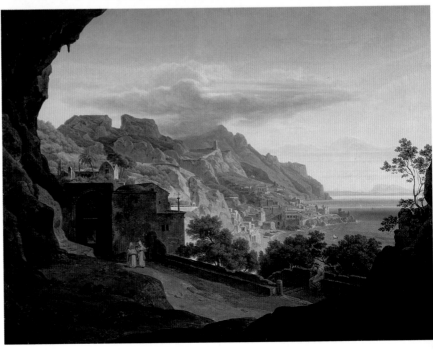

3

Jakob Philipp Hackert
Prenzlau 1737 – 1807 San Pietro di
Careggi
Lake Averno, 1794, signed and dated
Paper, 57.6 × 83.6 cm
Inv. no. 10162. Acquired in 1936 from
a private collection.
According to a description in an exhibition catalogue of 1798, this depicts
'An accurate view of Lake Averno and
the Gulf of Baia, from the road which
leads from Pozzuoli to the Arco Felice
and ancient Cumae . . . in the foreground a flowering aloe . . . The lake
itself is formed by the collapsed crater
of a volcano. On its left bank we see
the ruins of the Temple of Apollo, and
in the distance the castle of Baia and
the beautiful mountain of Miseno. The
scene is represented in the radiance of
a clear morning.'

4

Josef Anton Koch
Obergibeln 1768 – 1839 Rome
Heroic landscape with rainbow, 1815,
signed and dated
Canvas, 188 × 171.2 cm
Inv. no. WAF 447. Acquired in 1850 by
Ludwig I.
This oil-painting, which Koch began
as early as 1804, is the most ambitious
of a group of very similar pictures.
Shortly after its completion, the
Munich Academy acquired it as a
model of landscape painting to instruct
its student artists.

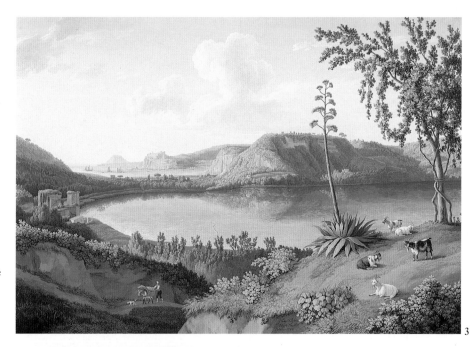

3

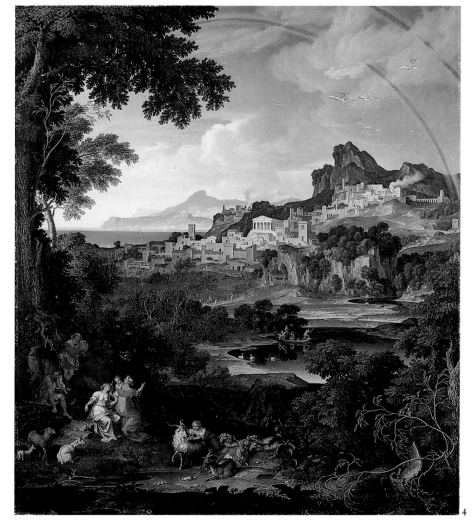

4

The Nazarenes

'Nazarenes' was the Italians' derisive nickname for the young German artists who, from
1810, lived as a quasi-monastic community in the former convent of Sant'Isidoro in Rome,
and grew their hair long in a manner reminiscent of Jesus of Nazareth. A group of them –
Friedrich Overbeck, Franz Pforr, Ludwig Vogel and Konrad Hottinger – had
previously been students at the Academy of Arts in Vienna, where in 1809 they had formed
a 'Lukasbund', or Brotherhood of St Luke, in deliberate recall of medieval tradition. In
opposition to the abstract, mechanical rules of the Academy's classicistic teaching, the
Brotherhood sought a specifically Christian and specifically German renewal of artistic
tradition. To this endeavour those who moved to Rome in the following year remained
true. In Rome they attracted several others to their circle, among them Giovanni Colombo,
the brothers Rudolf and Wilhelm Schadow and Johannes and Philipp Veit, Peter Cornelius,
Julius Schnorr von Carolsfeld, Friedrich Olivier, Joseph Anton Koch and Joseph Führich.

Despite their rejection of academic classicism, the Nazarenes' ideals, and the style and
subject matter of their painting, did not in many ways depart very far from it – even in
their characteristic recourse to Raphael, and in their efforts to synthesize the antitheses
between German and Italian art. They had absorbed much, including their medievalist
nostalgia, their emphasis on Germanness in art, their admiration for Raphael and Dürer,
from writers of the previous generation, such as Bodmer, Breitinger, Herder and Goethe,
and artists such as J. H. W. Tischbein. However, a step further was taken when several of
them adopted Catholicism, though even this had parallel in the conversion of writers such
as Wackenroder and Tieck.

The essence of the Nazarene movement was its innocence, and its 'suffer the little
children' ideal of purity and tenderness. The Nazarenes sought to unmake the history of
art, and to escape its taint and corruption by return to first principles, as represented by
their 'divine' Raphael and their 'beloved' Dürer. Their paintings reflected their hearts and
minds, and their subjects were chosen or framed in such a way as to avoid reference to the
particular and the present, or indeed the real. It was not long before the eye-catching
simplicity of their work and its religious, moral and nationalist appeal had brought the
Nazarenes fame and success, and they continued to find increasing recognition. While still
in Rome they received major decorative commissions, in the Casa Bartholdy and the Casino
Massimo; others, including Ludwig's in Munich, followed in Germany. They remained a
significant force in German art throughout the nineteenth century. The influence can
also be traced in France in the 1830s (on men such as Lamennais, Lacordaire and
Montalembert) and again at the end of the century on Gauguin and the Nabis (especially
Maurice Denis), and in England on the Pre-Raphaelites (artists such as Hunt, Millais,
Rossetti); it still largely affects popular religious art to this day.

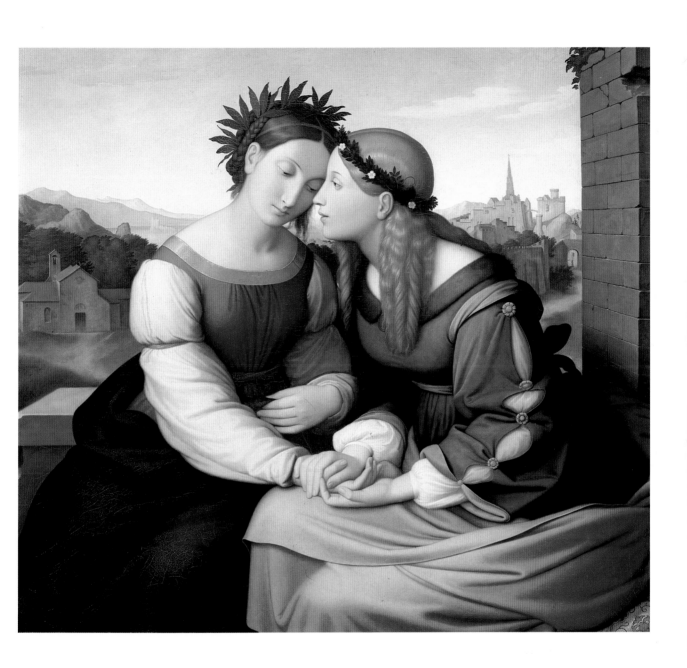

Johann-Friedrich Overbeck
Lubeck 1789 – 1869 Rome
Italia and Germania, 1828
Canvas, 94.4 × 104.7 cm
Inv. no. WAF 755. Acquired in 1832 by
order of Ludwig I, at its exhibition in
the Munich Academy.

Overbeck designed this painting, one
of the key works of the Nazarenes, as
an expression of his friendship for
Franz Pforr, who completed its pendant, *Sulamith and Maria*, shortly

before his early death. At that time,
Overbeck had only finished the cartoon, and produced the final version
only in 1828 for Wenner, a dealer in
books and art.

The picture is an allegory, and a
typical Nazarene subject, of the
union between Germany and Italy.
Both the imitation of Raphael's style
and the painting's delicacy are also
characteristic of the Nazarenes.

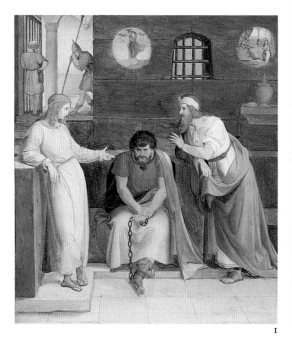

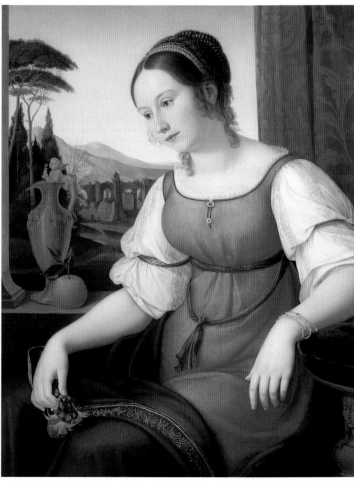

1

Friedrich Wilhelm von Schadow
Berlin 1788–1862 Düsseldorf
Joseph interpreting dreams, 1812
Board, 35 × 31 cm
Inv. no. 9408. Acquired in 1927 on the
Munich art market.
This is the scene (Genesis 40, 12f) in
which Joseph interprets the butler's
and baker's dreams whilst in prison.
Schadow used the design for one of
the murals in the Casa Bartholdy,
Rome.

2

Friedrich Wilhelm von Schadow
Berlin 1788–1862 Düsseldorf
A young Roman woman, 1818
Canvas, 94.3 × 73.1 cm
Inv. no. L267. Commissioned by
Crown Prince Ludwig. On loan from
the Verwaltung der staatlichen
Schlösser, Gärten und Seen, Munich
(Residenzmuseum Munich)

3

Johann-Friedrich Overbeck
Lübeck 1789–1869 Rome
Vittoria Caldoni da Albano, 1821
Canvas, 89 × 65.5 cm
Inv. no. WAF 757. Acquired in 1823 by
Crown Prince Ludwig.
The sitter was the daughter of a wine-
grower from Albano. She had her por-
trait painted by numerous artists,
especially the Nazarenes, for her face
embodied their ideal of beauty.

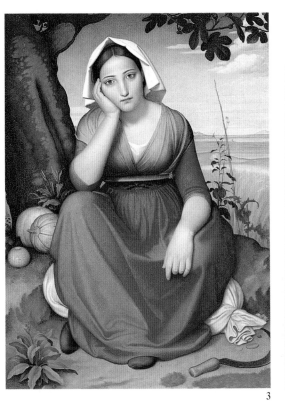

3

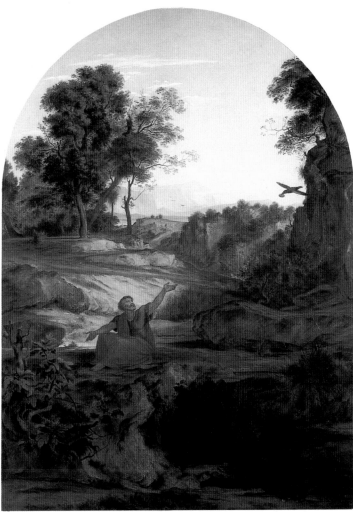

4

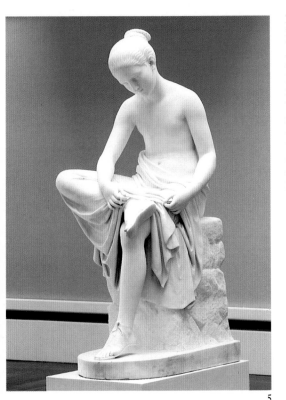

5

4
Ferdinand Olivier
Dessau 1785 – 1841 Munich
Elijah in the desert, 1830-31
Canvas, 75 × 56 cm
Inv. no. 9957. Acquired in 1934 on the Munich art market.
The picture represents I Kings 17, 4-6, in which Elijah prophesied a lengthy drought to King Ahab. Elijah himself was sent by God to the brook of Cherith and was fed bread and meat by ravens. There is also a study for this landscape in the Neue Pinakothek.

5
Rudolph (Ridolfo) Schadow
Rome 1786 – 1822 Rome
Woman tying her sandal, 1813 (1817), signed and dated
Marble, 118 cm high
Inv. no. WAF-B.24. Acquired by Crown Prince Ludwig I.
For this figure, Schadow combined naturalism with the evocation of famous antique sculptures such as the *spinario* or the *fanciulla* (a seated nymph) in the Uffizi, Florence. It was so successful with his contemporaries that he had to make seven replicas of it, of which this is one.

1

Heinrich Maria Hess
Düsseldorf 1798 – 1863 Munich
Marchesa Florenzi, 1824
Canvas, 192 × 139 cm
Inv. no. WAF 345. Commissioned by
Crown Prince Ludwig and acquired in
1824.

Hess painted this portrait on commission from Crown Prince Ludwig, the
future King Ludwig I, who had made
the acquaintance of the Marchesa
Marianna Florenzi in 1821 in Rome.
From that time, a very close relationship developed between them,
accompanied by a voluminous corres-
pondence. Ludwig also commissioned
other artists, including Joseph Karl
Stieler and Berthel Thorvaldsen, to
make portraits of the woman he so
much admired.

2

Friedrich Olivier
Dessau 1791 – 1859 Dessau
*The Loisachtal, c*1842-45
Canvas, 20 × 30 cm
Inv. no. 8968. Gift of Hugo Helbing,
1918.

In this oil-painting, the Loisachtal,
near Lake Kochel in Upper Bavaria, is
depicted.

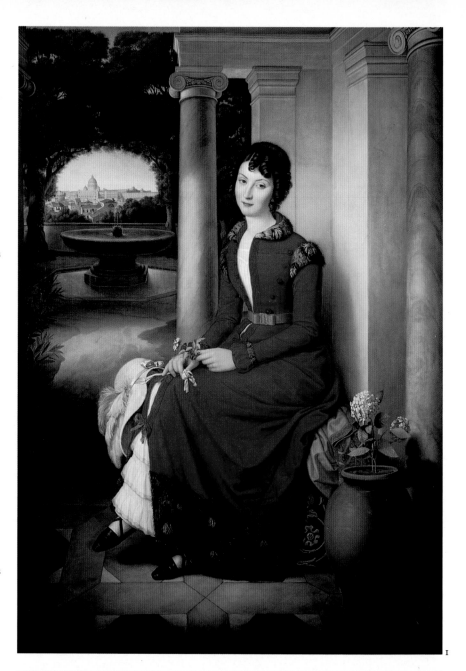

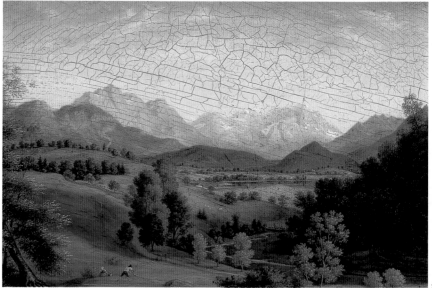

The Georg Schäfer collection

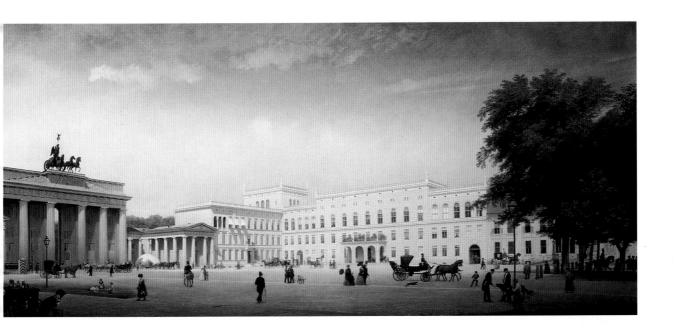

Eduard Gaertner
Berlin 1801 – 1877 Berlin
The Brandenburger Tor in Berlin with the north side of the Pariser Platz, 1846, signed and dated
Canvas, 60 × 130 cm
Inv. no. L.1833. On loan from the collection of Georg Schäfer, Schweinfurt

On the opening of the rebuilt Neue Pinakothek in 1981, a loan was arranged from the Georg Schäfer collection in Schweinfurt to the Bayerische Staatsgemäldesammlungen of 36 important paintings. The Schäfer paintings felicitously complement the Gallery's collection with works of a different character or by artists not represented in the State collections. The works concerned are all German or Austrian paintings of the nineteenth century, the particular emphasis of the Schäfer collection.

The Schäfer loan includes, of the Dresden 'school', works by Caspar David Friedrich and Carl Gustav Carus. Friedrich's paintings are sea-scapes and a *Vision of the Christian Church*, illustrating two aspects of his œuvre otherwise missing from the Gallery's holdings. There are outstanding pictures by Berlin artists, including paintings by Karl Blechen and a view of the Brandenburg Gate by Eduard Gaertner which has historical interest and is the only work by this architectural painter in the Gallery. There are also works by painters born or domiciled in Austria such as Ferdinand Waldmüller, Friedrich Wasmann and Friedrich von Amerling (notably his *Self-portrait*, 1843), significantly enhancing the Gallery's Biedermeier holdings.

Menzel, Leibl and their circle were already well represented in the Gallery, but the additional paintings from the Schäfer collection illustrate different stages of the artists' development and some, notably the portraits of Helene Auspitz, of Leibl's biographer Julius Mayer and of his friend and patron Geheimrat (Privy Councillor) Seeger, reveal facets of their intimate lives. Karl Schuch's *Still life* from the Schäfer collection fits chronologically between the Gallery's own *Still lifes*, one, of apples, of 1876 and the other of the mid-1880s, and is one of the artist's greatest achievements, commuting the simple presence of its ordinary subject. Menzel's early (1846) portrait of his brother Richard nicely complements the Museum's own holding of Menzel's intensely intimate works of this period.

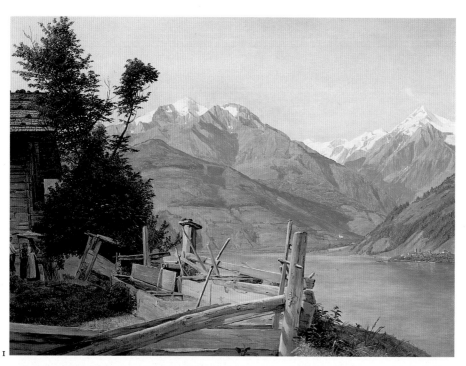

1

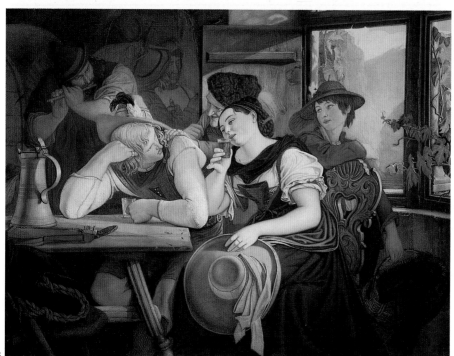

2

1
Ferdinand Georg Waldmüller
Vienna 1793–1865 Hinterbrühl
Zell am See in the Pinzgau, 1837,
signed and dated
Panel, 45 × 57 cm
Inv. no. L.1846. On loan from the
collection of Georg Schäfer,
Schweinfurt.
The view is from the eastern bank of
the lake facing Zell, with the Imbach-
horn to the left, the Wiesbachhorn in
the background, and the Kitzsteinhorn
on the right-hand edge of the picture.

2
Friedrich Wasmann
Hamburg 1805–1886 Meran
A Tyrolean tavern, 1847, signed and
dated
Canvas, 66.2 × 86.5 cm
Inv. no. L.1860. On loan from the
collection of Georg Schäfer,
Schweinfurt

3
Caspar David Friedrich
Greifswald 1774–1840 Dresden
Moonlit night with ships on the Baltic,
*c*1816-18
Canvas, 22.5 × 31.5 cm
Inv. no. L.1832. On loan from the
collection of Georg Schäfer,
Schweinfurt.
The pendant to this picture is a *Moon-*
lit night on the shores of the Baltic,
which is also in the Schäfer collection,
and on loan to the Neue Pinakothek.

4
Carl Gustav Carus
Leipzig 1789–1869 Dresden
The cemetery at Inning (so-called),
*c*1822
Canvas, 21.5 × 28.8 cm
Inv. no. L.1828. On loan from the
collection of George Schäfer,
Schweinfurt.
This is not in fact a picture of the
cemetery of Inning, near Lake
Ammer. The artist can only have
drawn inspiration from the grave
crosses he had seen in Bavaria for his
pictorial fantasy.

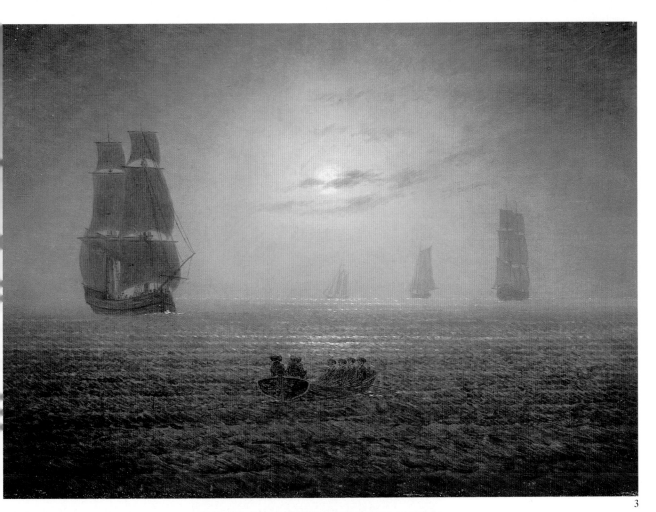

3

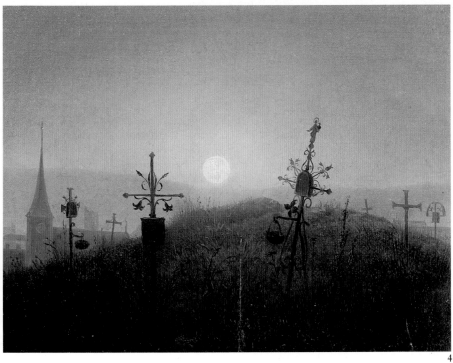

4

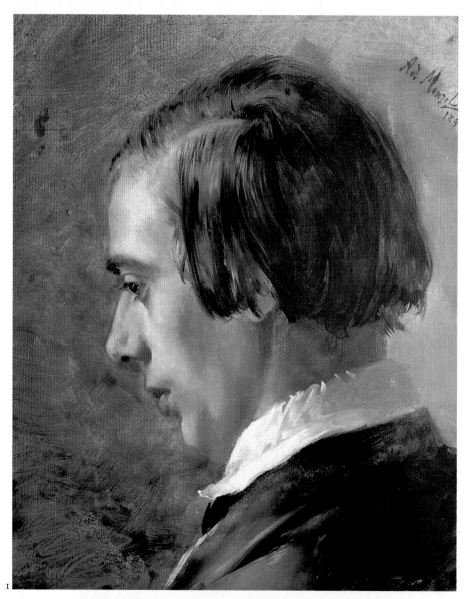

1

Adolph von Menzel
Breslau 1815 – 1905 Berlin
Richard Menzel, 1846, signed and
dated
Paper, 53.5 × 43 cm
Inv. no. L.1839. On loan from the
collection of Georg Schäfer,
Schweinfurt.
From the age of seventeen, after the
early death of his father, Menzel had
to support his family. He always took
an especially active interest in his brother Richard (1826-65), who found it
hard to make ends meet.

2

Adolph von Menzel
Breslau 1815 – 1905 Berlin
Wayside shrine near Salzburg, c1853,
signed
Canvas, 30.5 × 36 cm
Inv. no. L.1840. On loan from the
collection of Georg Schäfer,
Schweinfurt.

3

Wilhelm Leibl
Cologne 1844 – 1900 Würzburg
Frau Helene Auspitz, c1870-72
Canvas, 52 × 42 cm
Inv. no. L.1836. On loan from the
collection of George Schäfer,
Schweinfurt.
The subject of this oil-painting is the
first wife of the Viennese political
economist, Rudolf Auspitz. She lived
from 1836 to 1896 and as a painter was
known by her maiden name, Helen
von Lieben. Leibl began her portrait
while she was on a short visit to
Munich, and was invited by her to
transfer to Vienna.

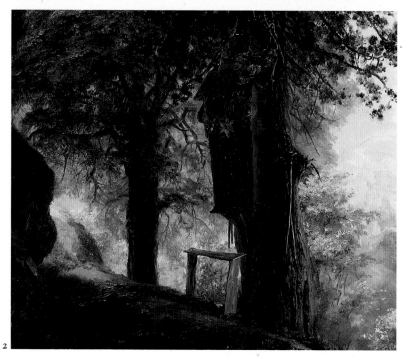

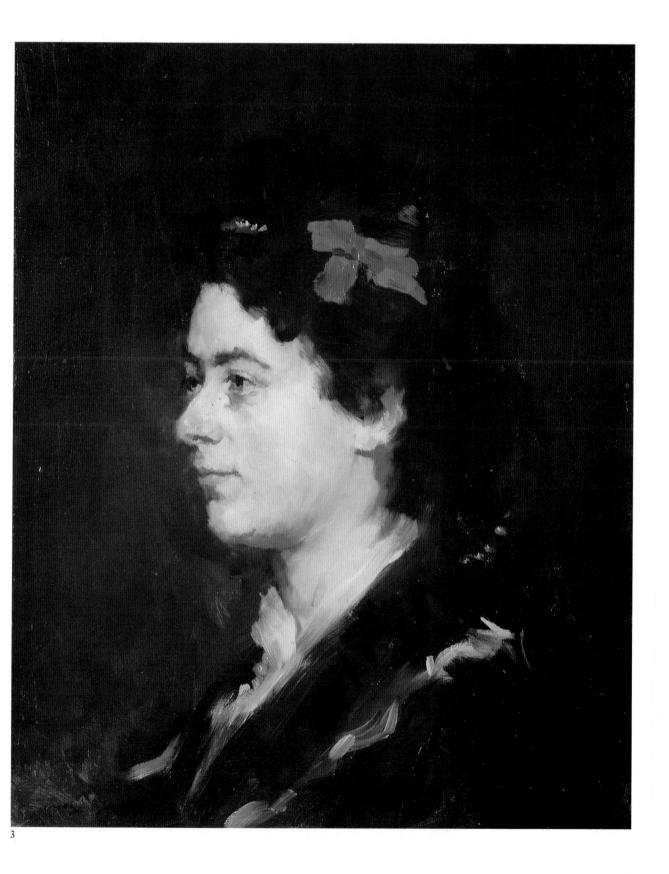

1
Wilhelm Leibl
Cologne 1844 – 1900 Würzburg
Geheimrat (Privy Councillor) Seeger
sitting on a chair, 1896, signed and
dated
Canvas, 102 × 78.5 cm
Inv. no. L.1835
On loan from the collection of George
Schäfer, Schweinfurt.
The Berlin art dealer and collector
Ernst Seeger had been Leibl's patron
and friend since 1895.

2
Carl Schuch
Vienna 1846 – 1903 Vienna
Still life with cheese-bell and game, 1885,
marked with a facsimile stamp
Canvas, 65.5 × 72.6 cm
Inv. no. L.1844. On loan from the
collection of Georg Schäfer,
Schweinfurt

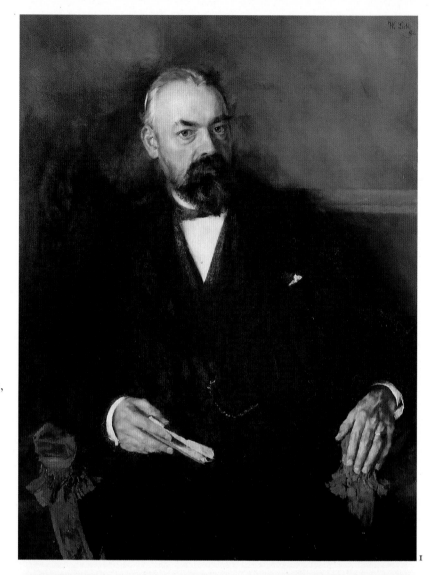

1

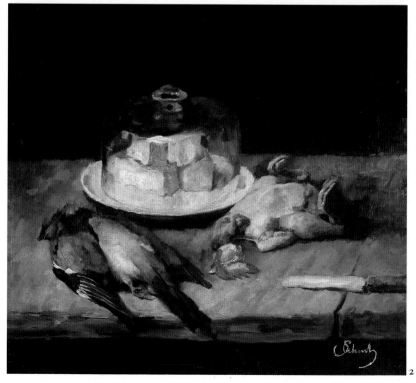

2

42

Sculpture

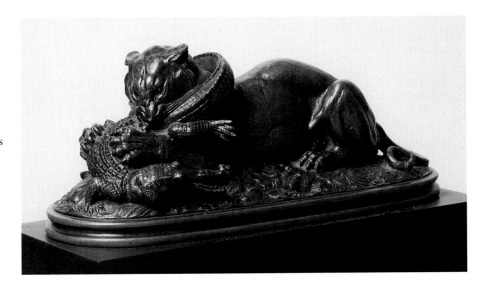

Paintings greatly outnumber sculptures in the Gallery's collection, but the Gallery's
holdings of sculpture include a remarkable, and sometimes truly outstanding range of
works dating from the end of the eighteenth century to the beginning of the twentieth.
They are to be found either in the rooms of the appropriate section or in the Gallery's
corridors, or in the annex which is devoted primarily to French, German and Italian
sculpture from the beginning to the end of the nineteenth century. The sculpture here is
mostly small-scale. The visitor is thereby enabled to recognise its development and
different aspects, and so achieve a basic, informative overview.

It contains works by Barye, known above all for his realistic sculptures of animals and
one of the most important animal sculptors of the century; neo-Baroque or neo-Rococo
figures by Carpeaux and Carrier-Belleuse; sculpture from the period of Impressionism and
Post-Impressionism by Rodin, Degas and Maillol, and *Jugendstil*, or Art Nouveau, work by
Franz von Stuck and Hermann Hahn.

Antonie-Louis Barye, a friend of Delacroix's, combined realistic depiction with a violent
temperament, so that his sculptures, usually groups of savage or ferocious animals, convey a
sense of the elemental side of nature. Jean-Baptiste Carpeaux and Albert-Ernest Carrier-
Belleuse in the next generation preferred the human figure, Carpeaux specialising
in group compositions or *tableaux*, Carrier-Belleuse in portraits, especially busts.
Auguste Rodin, younger again, was both taught by Barye and for a time was with
Carrier-Belleuse as one of his many assistants. Neither, however, exerted as much influence
on this greatest sculptor of the nineteenth century as Michelangelo. By contrast Aristide
Maillol, who began his career as a painter, had no interest in dramatic action. He produced
calm, monumentally simple figures in static poses, influenced by the rather decorative
manner of Gauguin and his circle, and emanating a kind of Mediterranean serenity
consciously inspired by ancient Greek statuary.

The works on display include loans made available by the generosity of the Bayerische
Versicherungskammer (Bavarian Chamber of Insurance) of sculpture acquired on the
advice of the Bayerische Staatsgemäldesammlungen.

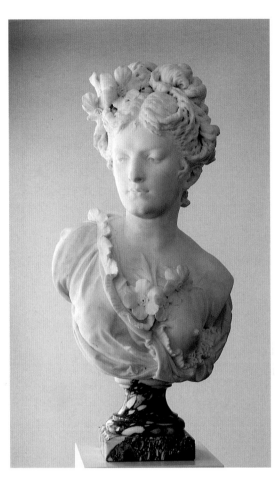

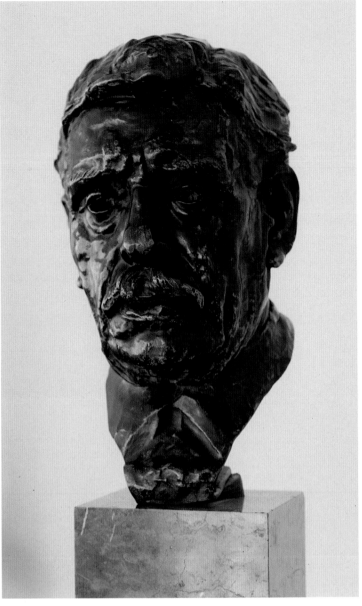

Albert-Ernest Carrier-Belleuse
Anizy-le-Château 1824–
1887 Sèvres
Female bust (*Flora*), signed
Marble, 60.2 cm high
Inv. no. B.777. Acquired in 1981 from
the Grünwald Gallery, Munich

Auguste Rodin
Paris 1840–1917 Meudon
Alexandre Falguière, 1899
Bronze, 44 cm high
Inv. no. B.67. Acquired in 1913 at the
Munich Glaspalast.
Alexandre Falguière (born Toulouse
1831, died Paris 1900) was a painter
and sculptor. He studied with Albert-
Ernest Carrier-Belleuse, Jean-Louis
Chenillon and François Jouffrey. His
first exhibition at the Salon was in
1857, and in 1859 he won the Prix de

Rome. In 1867, he came back to Paris,
and in the Salon of that year celebrated his greatest successes, which led to
a remarkably large number of commissions over the next few decades.
Although they were competitors for
the Balzac Monument, Rodin and Falguière maintained a relatively close
relationship. Rodin's bust of the older
sculptor had a counterpart in the portrait which Falguière sculpted of the
younger man.

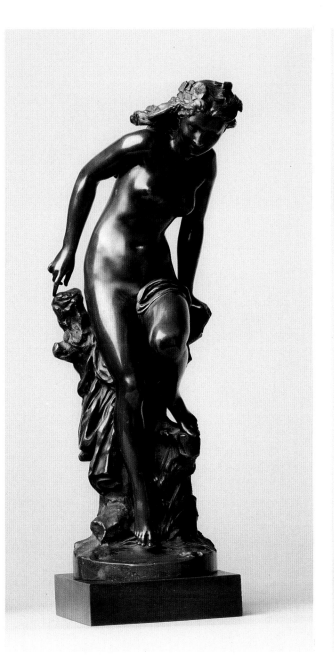

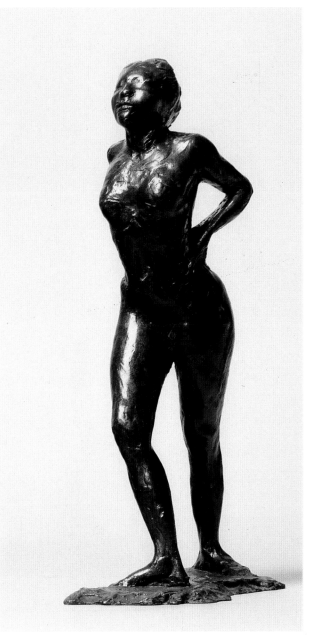

Jean-Baptiste Carpeaux
Valenciennes 1827–1875 Château
Bécon, near Asnières
'*La Frileuse*' (Catching cold), 1871,
signed
Bronze patinated golden brown,
40.8 cm high
Inv. no. L.1300. Acquired in 1971 for
the Bayerische Versicherungskammer,
Munich.
More versions of this figure exist also
in other materials.

Edgar Degas
Paris 1834–1917 Paris
Dancer at rest, c1880-90, signed
Bronze, 44.5 cm high
Inv. no. L.1748. On loan from a
private collection.
As well as oil-paintings, drawings and
printed graphics, Degas also created an
important body of sculptures, of which
over 70 survive.

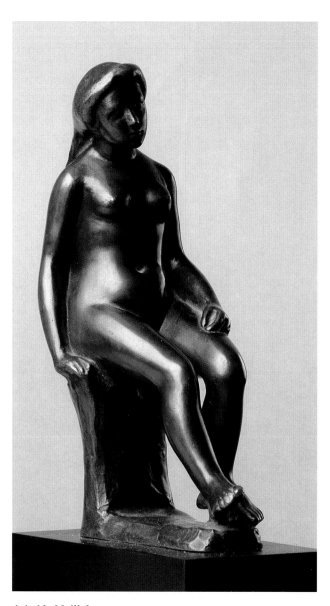

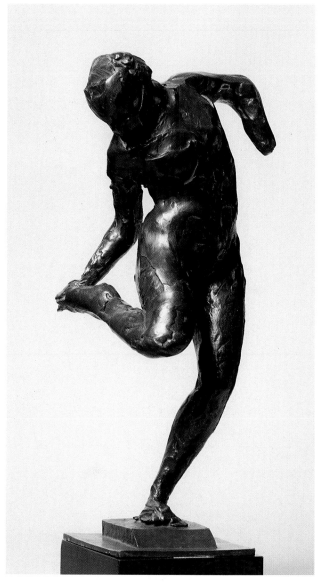

Aristide Maillol
Banyuls-sur-Mer 1861 –
1944 Banyuls-sur-Mer
Seated nude, 1907, signed
Bronze, 23 cm high (including base)
Inv. no. L.1745. On loan from a
private collection

Edgar Degas
Paris 1834 – 1917 Paris
Dancer, c1890-1900, signed
Bronze, 45 cm high
Inv. no. B.134. Acquired in 1929 on
the Munich art market

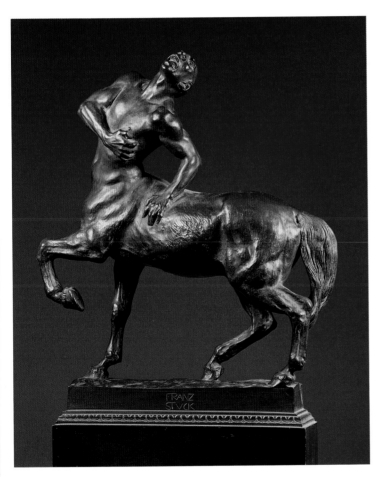

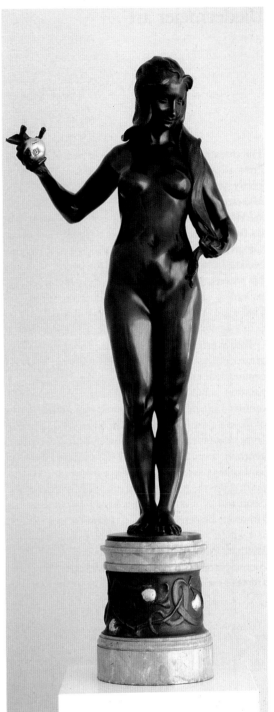

Franz von Stuck
Tettenweis 1863–1928 Munich
Wounded centaur, c1895-1900, signed
Bronze, 36.5 cm high, including base
Inv. no. B.25. Acquired in 1904 at the
Deutsche Künstlerbund exhibition in
Munich

Hermann Hahn
Kloster-Veilsdorf 1868–
1942 Munich
Eve, 1895, signed
Bronze, partially gilt, on a marble
base, 51 cm high including base
Inv. no. B.4. Acquired in 1905 at the
Munich Sezession exhibition

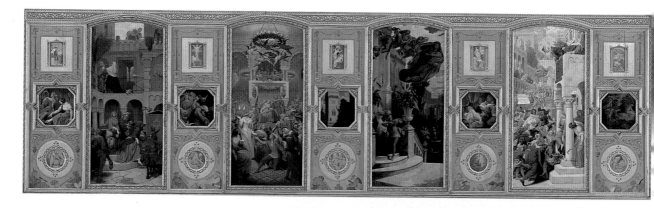

1
Moritz von Schwind
Vienna 1804 – 1871 Niederpöcking
The tale of Cinderella, 1852-54, signed
and dated
Canvas in a painted wooden frame,
151.5 × 480 cm
Inv. no. L.841. On loan from the
Bundesrepublik Deutschland.
The large panels, together with the
octagonal ones between them, tell the
story of Cinderella; the upper rectan-
gular panels in the intermediate sections, the story of Cupid and Psyche;
and the circular pictures below, the
story of Snow White.

2
Moritz von Schwind
Vienna 1804 – 1871 Niederpöcking
The visit, c1855
Canvas, 72 × 51 cm
Inv. no. 8120. Acquired in 1900 from
the artist's estate.
This painting is one of the artist's so-
called 'travel pictures', small-scale
works which Schwind produced in the
1850s and 1860s, while he had no pur-
chasers for his large pictures.

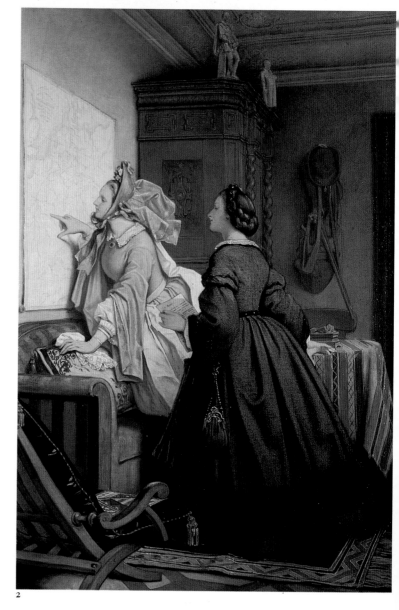

2

3

Ferdinand Georg Waldmüller
Vienna 1793 – 1865 Hinterbrühl
Ferdinand Waldmüller with a dog,
1836, signed and dated
Panel, 39.2 × 31.2 cm
Inv. no. 9274. Acquired in 1925 on the
Vienna art market.
The artist's son Ferdinand was born
in Brünn in 1816, and died in Vienna
in 1885.

4

Ferdinand Georg Waldmüller
Vienna 1793 – 1865 Hinterbrühl
Early spring in the Wienerwald, c1860,
signed and dated
Panel, 54.2 × 67.9 cm
Inv. no. 9324. Acquired in 1926 on the
Munich art market.
The picture belongs to a group of very
similar subjects by Waldmüller.

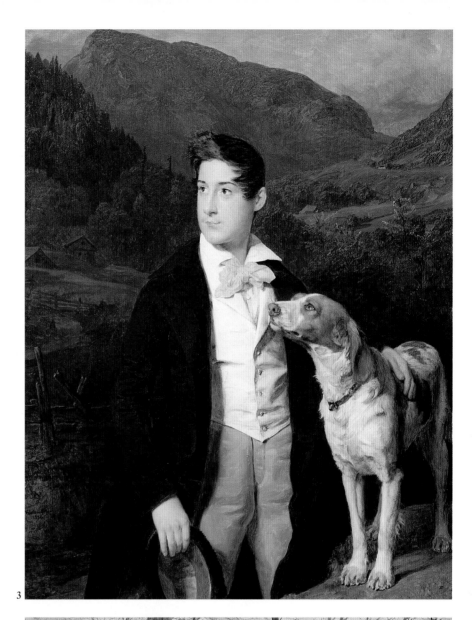

3

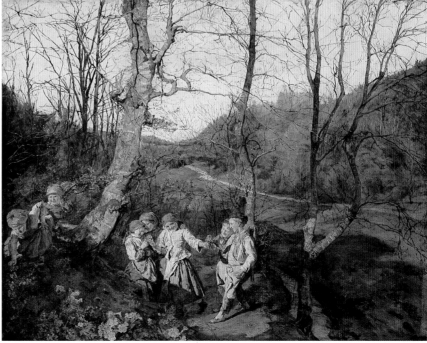

4

1
Domenico Quaglio
Munich 1787 –
1837 Hohenschwangau
The Old Riding School with the Café
Tambosi in 1822, 1822, signed and
dated
Canvas, 62 × 83 cm
Inv. no. WAF 786. Acquired by
Ludwig I.
The painting depicts the entrance into
the Ludwigstrasse in Munich during
its construction, looking north. In the
left foreground part of the façade of
the Theatine church is visible with the
so-called Lyre, or Lion Fountain, in
front of it. In the right background,
the Old Riding School, which was
demolished in 1822, and the Baroque
Café Tambosi at the Hofgarten can be
seen.

2
Friedrich von Amerling
Vienna 1803 – 1887 Vienna
Girl in a straw hat, c1835
Canvas, 59 × 47 cm
Inv. no. 9999. Acquired in 1935 on the
Munich art market.
This fine example of the Viennese
school of Biedermeier painting exists
in several autograph versions.

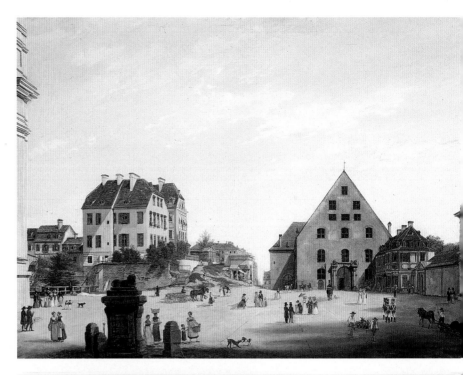

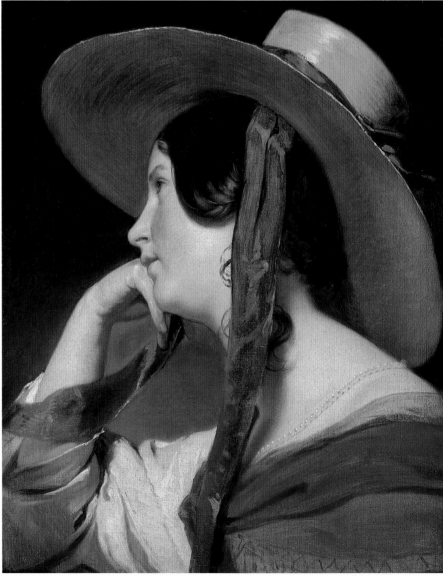

Late Romanticism and Realism in France

The important works exhibited in this section are extremely varied, and comparatively few of them are embraced by the term 'Romantic'. All, however, date from the early and middle nineteenth century, and most were in their own day progressive, that is, they were not Academic or produced by Academicians, and in one way or another they anticipated elements of Impressionism.

Théodore Géricault and Eugène Delacroix were painters of complex, eventful 'history' compositions of a kind that had no further development after Delacroix's death. Delacroix, the most important painter of the nineteenth century after Goya, was fully conscious of his own place as the heir to a long and rich tradition, but his works, though full of references to his artistic, literary and musical heritage, were innovative products of a personal vision and a passionate 'temperament'. Delacroix's handling of colour was a greater formative influence on the Impressionists than anyone else's, although their direct precursors were the painters of the Barbizon School – including Jean-Baptiste-Camille Corot, Gustave Courbet and Narcisse Diaz de la Peña.

Inspired by seventeenth-century Dutch painting and early nineteenth-century English painting, the Barbizon painters sought with new rigour to represent landscape as it was, unadulterated and unglamourised. Their honesty and realism influenced not only the French Impressionists but many other artists including Van Gogh and Liebermann, and transformed the depiction not only of landscape but also of its inhabitants – in Van Gogh's work or in that of Jean-François Millet. While Millet rendered peasants as heroes, even glorified them, the painter and caricaturist Honoré Daumier mirrored social conditions in a sharper, more disagreeable focus. The two paintings in the Gallery by Daumier are among his most famous. Auguste Rodin's work is also exhibited in other rooms, but this section is the home of his *Man with a broken nose*, a masterpiece and a kind of metaphorical self-portrait, which also recalls classical heads of Greek philosophers, and for which the actual sitter was a worker in the Paris horse market. Its realism and at the same time its resonance illustrate Rodin's exceptional range and power, much greater than the term 'Impressionism' in its usual sense can cover.

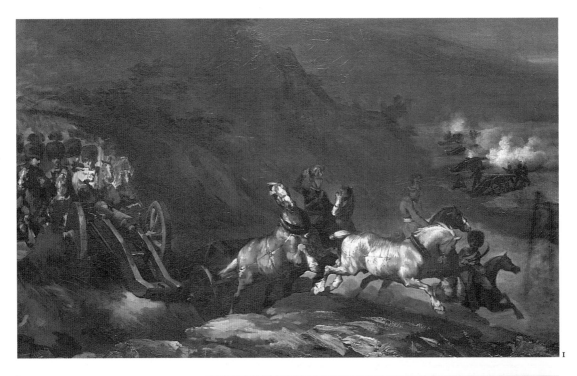

1

Théodore Géricault
Rouen 1791 – 1824 Paris
Bringing artillery to bear, c1814
Canvas, 89.2 × 143.7 cm
Inv. no. 8583. Acquired in 1910 on the
Berlin art market

2

Théodore Géricault
Rouen 1791 – 1824 Paris
Heroic landscape with fishermen, 1818,
signed
Canvas, 249.5 × 217.5 cm
Inv. no. 14561. Acquired in 1978 on
the New York art market.
The 'staged' character of this picture is
explained by its original purpose as
wall decoration. Géricault painted this
and two companion pieces in 1818, for
a room in his friend Marceau's house
at Villers-Cotterets, near Paris.

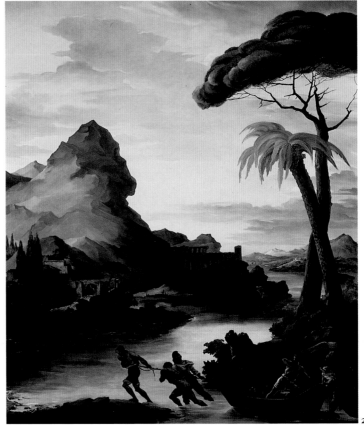

Eugène Delacroix
Charenton-St Maurice 1798–
1863 Paris
Clorinde frees Olindo and Sofronia,
1853–56, signed
Canvas, 101 × 82 cm
Inv. no. 13165. Acquired in 1962 from

a private collection in London.
This depicts a scene from the second
canto of *Gerusalemme Liberata* by Tor-
quato Tasso (1544–95), which has as its
subject the conquest of Jerusalem
during the First Crusade in 1099. In
Tasso's poem the Christian woman,

Sophronia, took a stolen picture of the
Virgin from the Mosque at Jerusalem,
and was condemned to the stake along
with her lover, Olindo. The chivalrous
Saracen woman Chlorinde freed them
both, and persuaded the Sultan to
pardon them.

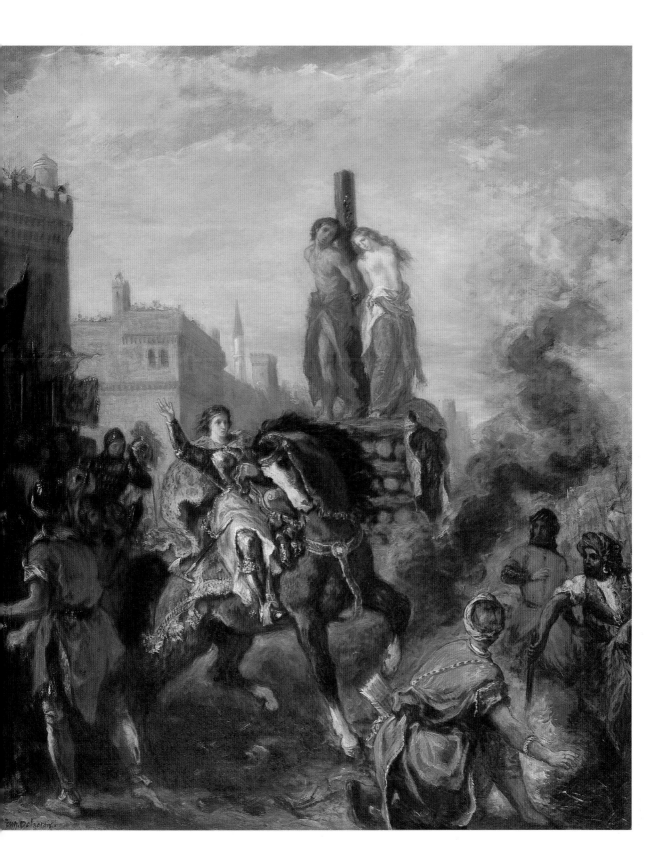

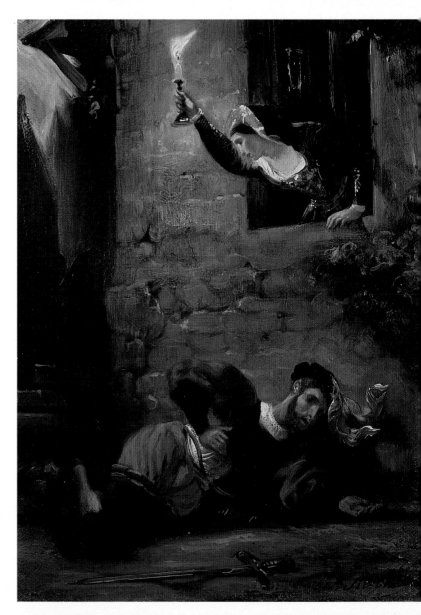

1
Eugène Delacroix
Charenton-St Maurice 1798–
1863 Paris
The death of Valentin, c1830, signed
Canvas, 32.5 × 24.3 cm
Inv. no. 14248. Bequeathed in 1971 by
Theodor and Woty Werner.
The painting depicts a scene from
Goethe's *Faust* I (lines 3712f), when
Valentin, Gretchen's brother, dies
after the duel with Faust and
Mephisto. Delacroix had earlier seen
Retzsch's *Faust* illustrations, but what
most impressed him was an opera
production in 1825 in London. As
well as a number of oils, the artist
subsequently produced some lithographs on the theme. These were published in 1828 and Goethe himself
thought highly of them.

2
Eugène Delacroix
Charenton-St Maurice 1798–
1863 Paris
The death of Ophelia, 1838, signed
Canvas, 37.9 × 45.9 cm
Inv. no. 12764. Acquired in 1958 from
a private collection in Switzerland.
Delacroix has depicted the death of
Ophelia from *Hamlet* (Act IV, Scene 7):
There is a willow grows aslant a brook,
That shows his hoar leaves in the glassy stream;
There, with fantastic garlands did she come,
Of crow-flowers, nettles, daisies, and long purples,
That liberal shepherds give a grosser name,
But our cold maids do dead men's fingers call them,
There, on the pendant boughs her coronet weeds
Clambering to hang, an envious sliver broke;
When down the weedy trophies, and herself,
Fell in the weeping brook. Her clothes spread wide,
And, mermaid-like, a while they bore her up:
Which time, she chanted snatches of old tunes;
As one uncapable of her own distress,
Or like a creature native and indued
Unto that element: but long it could not be,
Till that her garments, heavy with their drink,
Pull'd the poor wretch from her melodious lay
To muddy death.
The artist depicted the same scene in
two other versions (now in Paris and
Winterthur). The *Hamlet* lithographs
which he produced between 1834-43
also show how important Shakespeare
was to Delacroix.

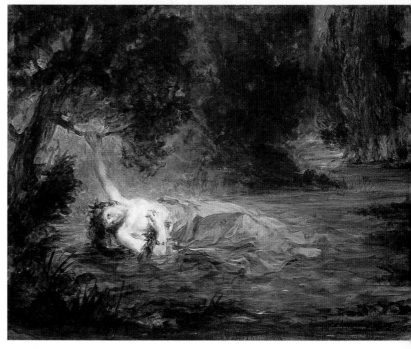

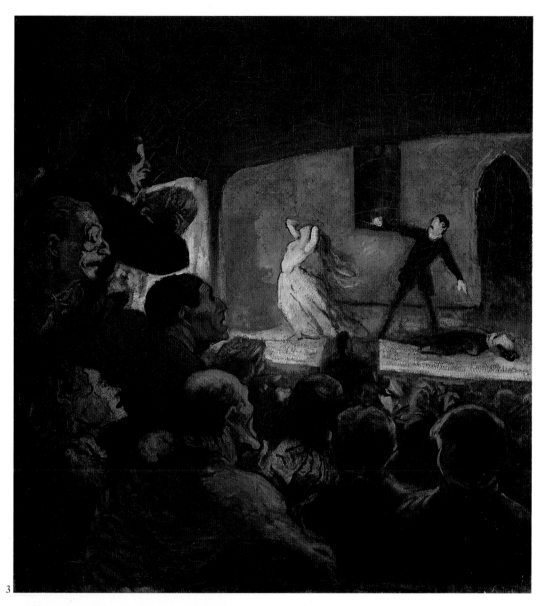

3

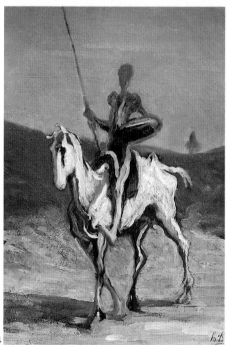

4

3
Honoré Daumier
Marseilles 1808–1879 Valmondois
The play, c1860, signed
Canvas, 97.5 × 90.4 cm
Inv. no. 8697. Gift of Reichsrat
Theodor Freiherr von Cramer-Klett in
1913 as part of the Tschudi donation.

4
Honoré Daumier
Marseilles 1808–1879 Valmondois
Don Quixote, c1868, signed
Canvas, 52.2 × 32.8 cm
Inv. no. 8698. Gift of Karl Sternheim
in 1913 as part of the Tschudi
donation.
Daumier depicted the hero of Cer-
vantes's novel in a number of paintings
produced from the early 1850s
onwards. The work in Munich is a
preparatory study for the painting now
in Boston.

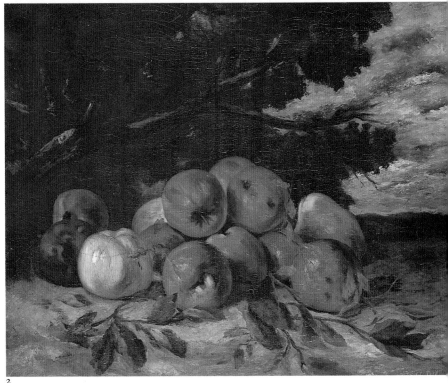

1

Gustave Courbet
Ornans 1819–1877 La Tour de Peilz
The lock at Optevoz, 1854(?), signed
Canvas, 63.6 × 84.5 cm
Inv. no. 8584. Acquired in 1910 on the Paris art market.
Courbet and Charles-François Daubigny first painted in the Optevoz region (Isère) in 1854. Daubigny also represented the same scene in a number of pictures.

2

Gustave Courbet
Ornans 1819–1877 La Tour de Peilz
Still life of apples, 1871, signed
Canvas, 50.4 × 63.4 cm
Inv. no. 8623. Gift of M. von Nemes in 1911.
Courbet produced this picture in Ste-Pélagie prison, where he was serving a sentence for his part in the destruction of the Column in the Place Vendôme in Paris.

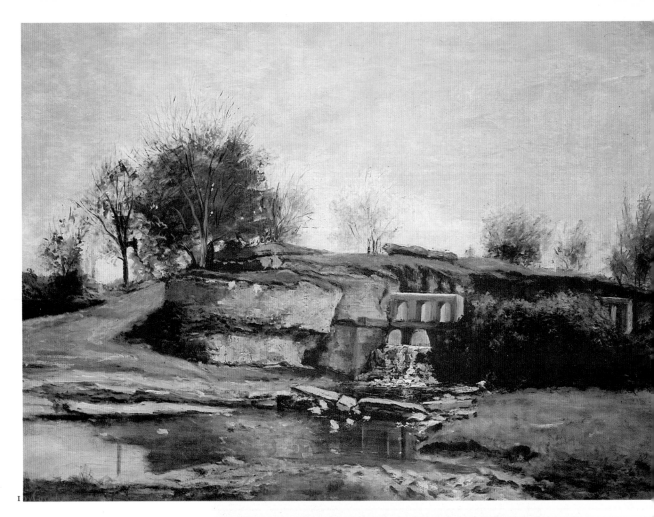

2

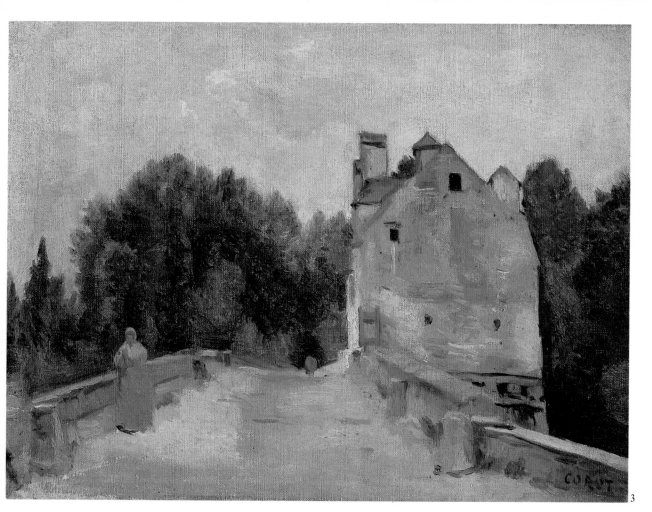

3

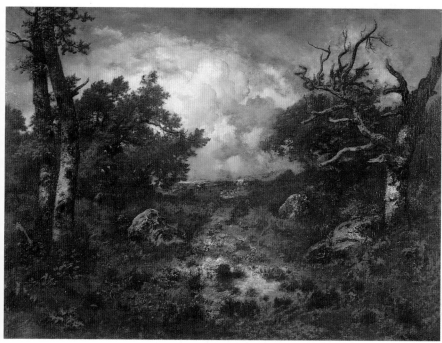

3
Camille Corot
Paris 1796 – 1875 Paris
The bridge and the mill in Mantes
('Mantes – l'entrée du pont'),
*c*1860, signed
Canvas, 25.5 × 33 cm
Inv. no. 8844. Acquired in 1915 on the
Munich art market.
After 1855, Corot made frequent visits
to Mantes, north-west of Paris, where
he painted a number of pictures.

4
Narcisse Diaz de la Peña
Bordeaux 1809 – 1876 Menton
A glade in the forest of Fontainebleau,
1868, signed and dated
Canvas, 83.3 × 112.1 cm
Inv. no. 12523. Transferred from State
ownership in 1957

4

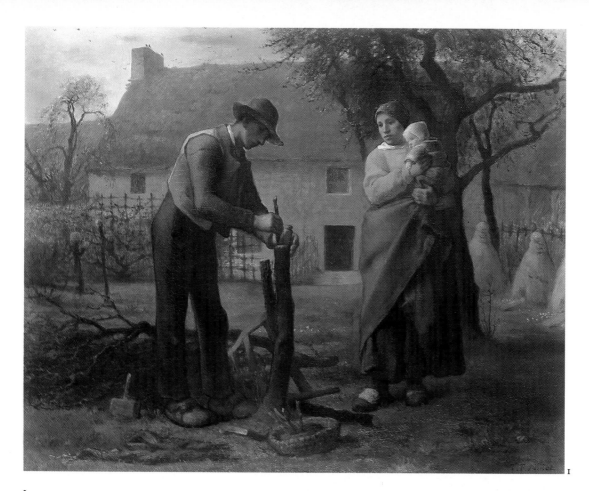

1
Jean-François Millet
Gruchy 1814–1875 Barbizon
Grafting ('Le Greffeur'), 1855, signed
Canvas, 80.5 × 100 cm
Inv. no. 14556. Acquired in 1978 on
the New York art market.
In this picture, the analogy between
the new growth and the small child is
part of the symbolism which charac-
terises Millet, and which made a deep
impression on Vincent van Gogh, on
whose painting in general Millet was
greatly influential.

2
Auguste Rodin
Paris 1840–1917 Meudon
Man with a broken nose ('L' homme au
nez cassé'), 1863
Bronze, 30.5 cm high
Inv. no. L.209. Acquired in 1986 for
the Bayerische Versicherungskammer,
Munich.
In this head, Rodin combined the
ancient poet and philosopher bust-
type with realistic study from life. He
also makes reference to Daniele da
Volterra's portrait of Michelangelo.
This early cast may have come from
the collection of the poet Robert
Browning.

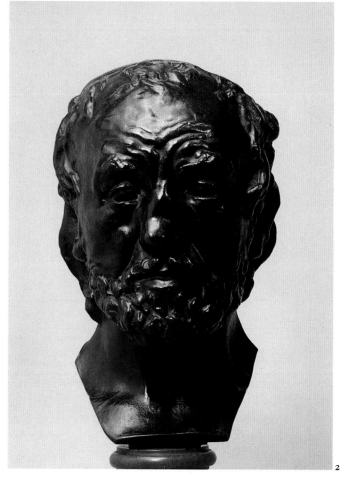

Late Romanticism and Realism in Germany

Three very important 'schools' of German painting in the nineteenth century are represented in this section – Berlin, Düsseldorf and Munich. The leading figure, one of the greatest German artists of the whole period, is Adolph von Menzel, who spent most of his long career in Berlin. Menzel's distinctive graphic gifts and narrative skill early found expression in his illustrations to Kugler's *History* of Frederick the Great (1839-42), and numerous subsequent paintings reflect a virtual obsession with Prussia's age of glory – one that only increased after the creation of the First Reich in 1871. Menzel, however, represented scenes from the period with considerable subtlety. He usually avoided the general fashion for military heroics, preferring social scenes or social occasions which he liked to enliven with anecdotal touches. He was always interested in the human and psychological side of history, and not surprisingly his enormous output also includes scenes of contemporary life, indeed depictions of virtually everything he might encounter. His works in this vein reveal not simply powers of observation but a surprisingly poetic eye; they are not mere literal representations. This is an aspect of his work that emerges most clearly in the sketches he made early in his career, during the 1840s, which were not intended for sale and which have an intensity and immediacy very different from the highly detailed, *raconteur* paintings of his later years.

Carl Spitzweg in Munich shared Menzel's penchant for anecdotal narrative, but his work has by contrast a sprinkling of mild irony, verging on virtual caricature. Spitzweg and his circle – Eduard Schleich, Dietrich Langko, Friedrich Voltz, Bernhard Stange and Christian Morgenstern – were nevertheless progressive artists, who, especially in their landscapes, reoriented their art to the guiding principle of truth to nature and who were abreast therefore with the latest trends in France (the Barbizon School) and England (Constable, Turner).

Three of the best-known artists in the Düsseldorf 'school' are exhibited, Johann Wilhelm Schirmer and his pupils Andreas and Oswald Achenbach. Düsseldorf being so close to Holland, its artists were strongly influenced by Dutch art, especially the dramatic nature studies of Jacob van Ruisdael and Allaert van Everdingen. Thus, in their own way, which soon brought them considerable recognition, these artists, too, participated in the general realist trend.

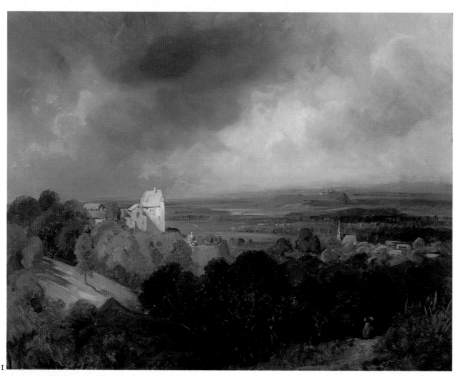

1

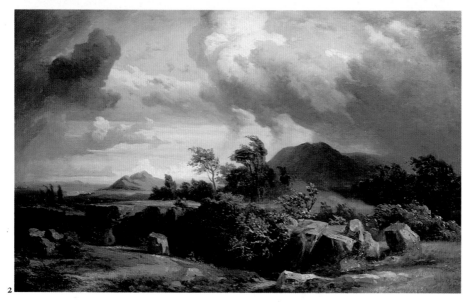

2

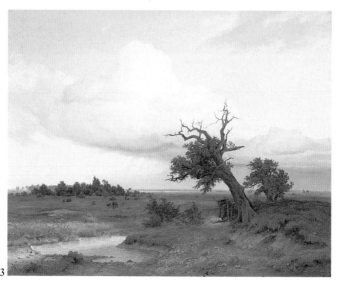

3

1
Eduard Schleich the Elder
Haarbach 1812 – 1874 Munich
*At Brannenburg, c*1850, signed
Panel, 30 × 38.7 cm
Inv. no. 8023. Bequeathed by the
painter Anton Höchl in 1897.
The castle and village of Brannenburg
lie north-west of Falkenstein on the
River Inn.

2
Johann Wilhelm Schirmer
Jülich 1807 – 1863 Karlsruhe
*Stormy evening, c*1860
Canvas, 38 × 60.5 cm
Inv. no. 9006. Acquired in 1919 from
the Heinemann Gallery, Munich.
This painting may have been inspired
by impressions of the Roman Camp-
agna experienced by Schirmer some
twenty years previously.

3
Eduard Schleich the Elder
Haarbach 1812 – 1874 Munich
Landscape with withered oak, 1832,
signed and dated
Canvas, 60.3 × 75.5 cm
Inv. no. 8544. Acquired in 1908 on the
Munich art market.
This is the earliest known painting by
Schleich.

4
Carl Spitzweg
Munich 1808 – 1885 Munich
The penniless poet, 1839, signed and
dated
Canvas, 36.2 × 44.6 cm
Inv. no. 7751. Gift of Eugen Spitzweg
in 1887.
There is a second version of the paint-
ing, very similar to this, produced in
the same year. In both pictures,
Spitzweg depicts a poet condemned to
failure through the inadequacy of his
talents with ironic humour.

5
Carl Spitzweg
Munich 1808 – 1885 Munich
The nature walk, 1872, signed
Canvas, 32.1 × 54.1 cm
Inv. no. 11995. Transferred from State
ownership in 1957

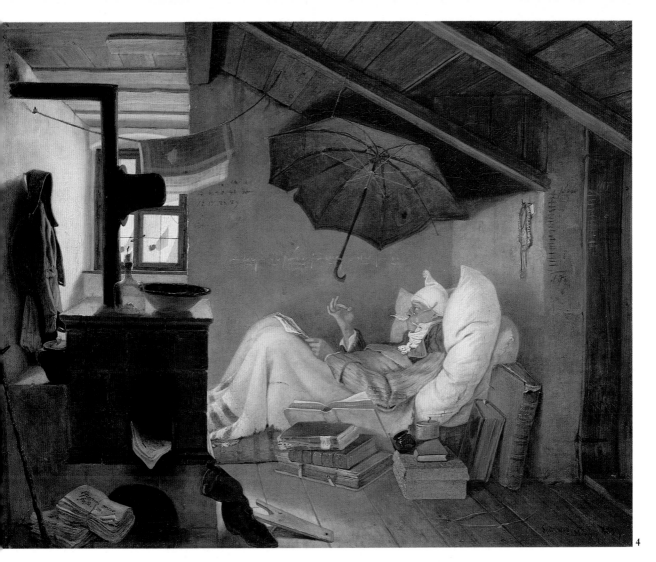

4

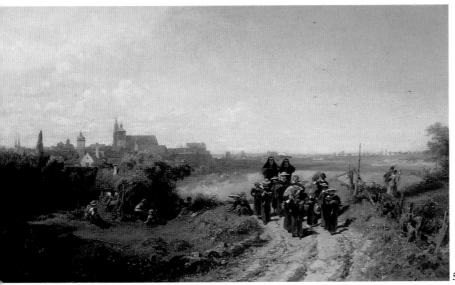

5

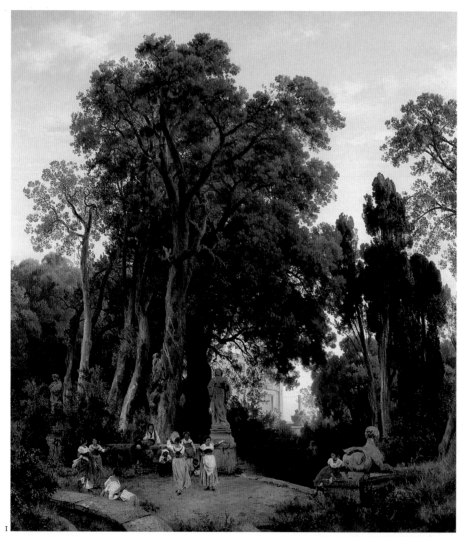

1

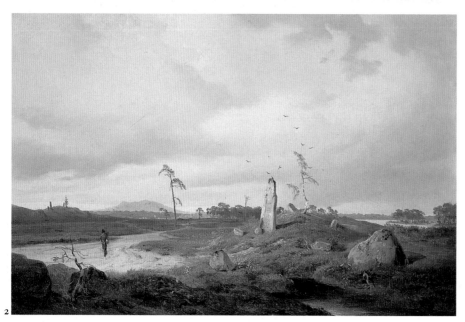

2

1
Oswald Achenbach
Düsseldorf 1827 – 1905 Düsseldorf
An Italian park, c1860, signed
Canvas, 130.3 × 116.3 cm
Inv. no. 12512. Transferred from State
ownership in 1957.
Oswald Achenbach, brother of
Andreas, in this painting recalls similar
motifs in pictures by Karl Blechen
(1798-1840).

2
Andreas Achenbach
Kassel 1815 – 1910 Düsseldorf
Landscape with rune-stone, 1841,
signed and dated
Canvas, 34.5 × 52 cm
Inv. no. 14599. Gift of the Allianz-
Versicherungs AG, Munich, in 1979.
This landscape, though painted on Mt
Eifel in western Germany, neverthe-
less probably reflects the artist's
impressions of Norway. The style is
reminiscent of the early German
Romantics, even though Achenbach is
more realistic.

3
Adolph von Menzel
Breslau 1815 – 1905 Berlin
Living room with the artist's sister,
1847, signed and dated
Paper, 46.1 × 31.6 cm
Inv. no. 8499. Acquired in 1937 from
the artist's niece, Margarethe Krigar-
Menzel.
The girl in the picture is Menzel's
younger sister, Emilie (born 1823),
with whom the artist had an especially
close relationship. After his sister's
marriage in 1859 to the Director of the
Royal Music, Hermann Krigar, the
couple set up a communal household
with Menzel, who was unmarried. In
the background, Menzel's mother is at
her sewing. Neither this nor other
similar early pictures made as sketches
were intended for exhibition.

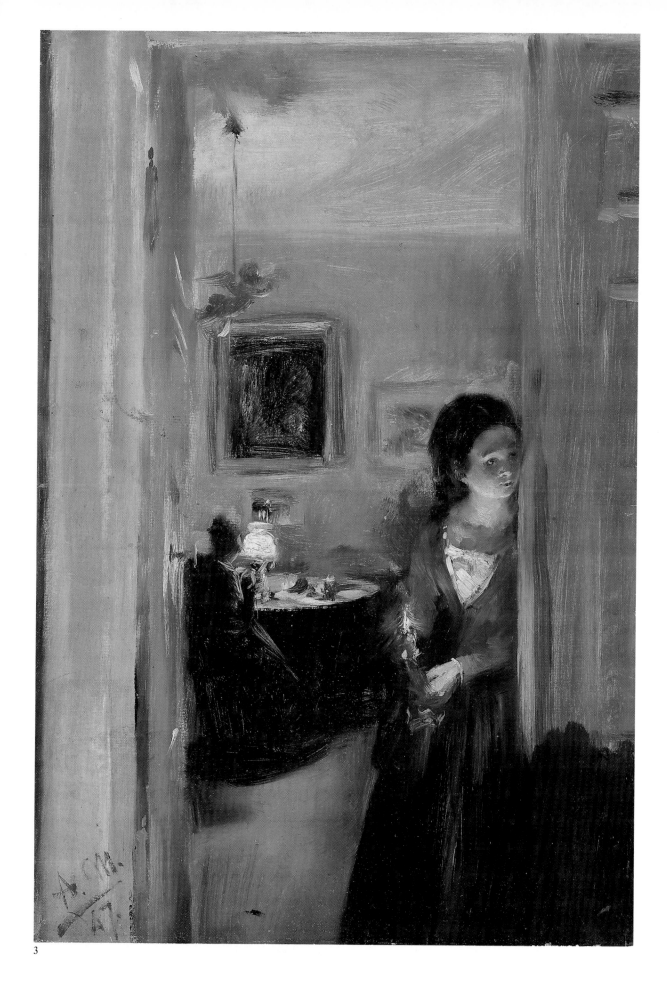

3

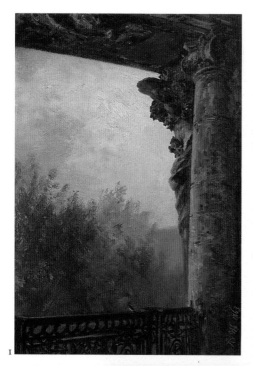

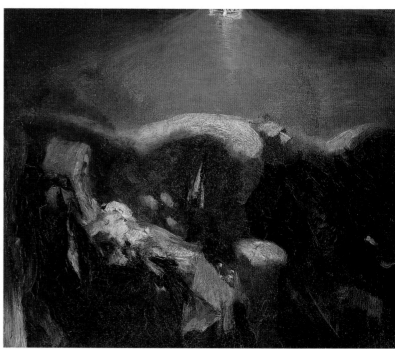

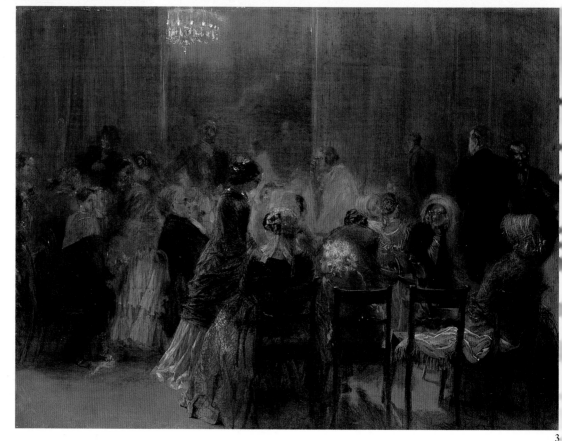

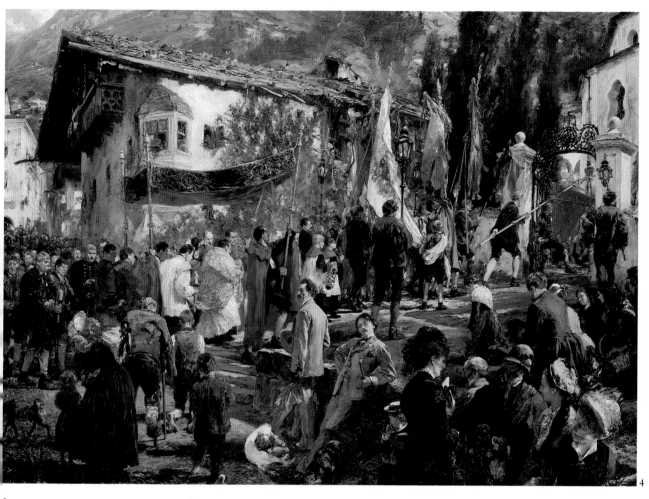

4

1
Adolph von Menzel
Breslau 1815–1905 Berlin
View from the Berliner Schloss, 1863,
signed and dated
Canvas, 52.6 × 37 cm
Inv. no. 8502. Acquired in 1937 from
the artist's niece, Margarethe Krigar-
Menzel

2
Adolph von Menzel
Breslau 1815–1905 Berlin
In the railway carriage compartment,
c1848
Canvas, 43.1 × 52.2 cm
Inv. no. 9880. Acquired in 1932 on the
Munich art market

3
Adolph von Menzel
Breslau 1815–1905 Berlin
Private concert, 1851, signed and dated
Gouache and pastel on paper,
mounted on panel, 44.7 × 58.9 cm
Inv. no. 8501. Acquired in 1937 from
the artist's niece, Margarethe Krigar-
Menzel

4
Adolph von Menzel
Breslau 1815–1905 Berlin
A procession in Hofgastein, 1880, signed
and dated
Canvas, 51.3 × 70.2 cm
Inv. no. L.817. On loan from the
Bundesrepublik Deutschland since
1966.
During the 1870s and 1880s, Menzel
often spent the summer in (Bad)
Hofgastein.

Wilhelm von Kaulbach's designs for the frescoes of the former Neue Pinakothek

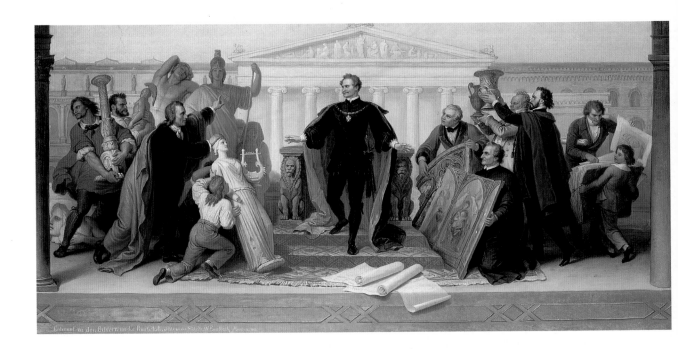

Wilhelm von Kaulbach's cartoons for the frescoes that once adorned the outside walls of the former Neue Pinakothek are exhibited in a long narrow room to themselves. The frescoes (on a much larger scale) of the now destroyed building soon deteriorated, and are recorded only in inadequate reproductions, so that the cartoons are now the best guide to Ludwig's intentions for his museum, which have considerable historical interest. The cartoons are exhibited in the following order:

East side (entrance front of the former Neue Pinakothek): Allegorical figures (1) of *Architecture*, *Stone sculpture* and *Bronze-casting*; (2) of *Fresco-painting*, *Glass-staining* and *Ceramics*.

South side (front of the former Neue Pinakothek facing the Alte Pinakothek): (3) *The defeat of the periwig or pigtail style, represented in the form of a three-headed monster, since this style has wrought havoc in all three Fine Arts*; (4) and (5) *German artists studying in Rome*; (6) *King Ludwig, surrounded by artists and scholars, descends from the throne to view the paintings and sculptures which they have presented to him*; (7) (8) and (9) *Painters, sculptors and architects summoned by King Ludwig*.

West side: (10) (11) and (12) *Glass-staining, bronze-casting and porcelain manufacture in Munich*.

North side: (13) *The artists and citizens of Munich present the King in 1850 with the 'King Ludwig Album'*; (14) (15) (16) (17) and (18) *Artists' portraits*; (19) *A festival of the arts in which a statue of King Ludwig is unveiled.*

History painting and establishment art in the 'Gründerzeit'

Wilhelm von Kaulbach
Arolsen 1804–1874 Munich
King Ludwig, surrounded by artists and scholars, descends from the throne to view the paintings and sculptures they have presented to him, 1848, signed and dated
Canvas, 78.5 × 163 cm
Inv. no. WAF 406.
This and eighteen other pictures were designs which Kaulbach prepared for a cycle of frescoes on the outside walls of the former Neue Pinakothek (*cf* illus. p.4). He produced the designs between 1848 and 1854. The full-scale frescoes were executed by Christoph Nilson between 1850 and 1854.
The theme that Ludwig I stipulated in the contract for the frescoes was:
'. . . recent developments in art . . . called into being by his Majesty, and originating from Munich'. He also expressly intended that the designs were to be placed inside the building. This design for the middle picture on the south wall depicts Ludwig I as an art collector, against a background of the Munich Glyptothek (centre), the Alte Pinakothek (left), and the State Library. Ancient and medieval works of art, as the two major areas of royal interest, are represented.

This section contains for the most part works of so-called 'official' art – that is, created by members and professors of the academies – dating from the *Gründerzeit*, or the years of Germany's industrial expansion in the second half of the nineteenth century. It also exhibits independent artists – such as Franz von Lenbach and Albert von Keller – whose work in a similar fashion satisfied the expectations and needs of the establishment. Such works served the purpose of 'Repräsentation' or status enhancement: many of them were public, that is 'history' paintings or sculpture for palaces and government buildings, churches, museums and so forth, and even if privately commissioned the remainder, largely portraits and group portraits, had in practice a semi-public function. These works were invariably historicist, echoing the formulae of the Italian Renaissance, Flemish Baroque and later Dutch painting, and thereby meeting the two main requirements of grandeur and monumentality.

During this period there opened (not only in Munich) a clear divide between two kinds of art, establishment or official art and another art, committed to nature, for which there was little or no official outlet. On one side stood artists such as Wilhelm and Friedrich August von Kaulbach, Karl von Piloty, Hans Makart, Keller and Lenbach, on the other men such as Leibl and his friends, Liebermann in his early career and Marées. This was a new development, though it was connected with the enormous social changes that had been initiated in the late eighteenth century. It is evident that a universal standard by which art could be assessed or judged no longer existed, and different criteria and values prevailed in different quarters.

In the Munich Akademie, under the directorships of Cornelius (1824-40), Kaulbach (1849-74) and Piloty (1874-86), the absolute priority of 'history painting' over genre-painting, portraiture, landscape and still life was never doubted; these artists felt themselves part of the Renaissance tradition, and their employers, pillars of the State and the Church, saw themselves as successors to the patrons of Raphael, Titian, Rubens or Van Dyck. In keeping with that tradition, they believed that the rôle of 'history painting' consisted not merely in decoration on a grand scale, but in the representation of relevant contemporary subjects, and especially subjects significant for national identity. In Munich, the grand tradition could be seen to have come to an end with Piloty's pupil Franz von Defregger, in whose rather few 'history paintings' the element of genre – of the kind that had long been popular in Munich – becomes predominant.

Thus this section also contains Defregger's sentimental genre pieces, Keller's elegant society gatherings, and aristocratic portraits by Keller, Lenbach and Friedrich August von Kaulbach. In the last third of the nineteenth century literal and naturalistic realism became acceptable in official art, hence the works displayed here by Eduard Schleich, Adolf Lier, Dietrich Langko and Joseph Wenglein. These men, though not involved in the Akademie, had a considerable following, including Leibl and his circle.

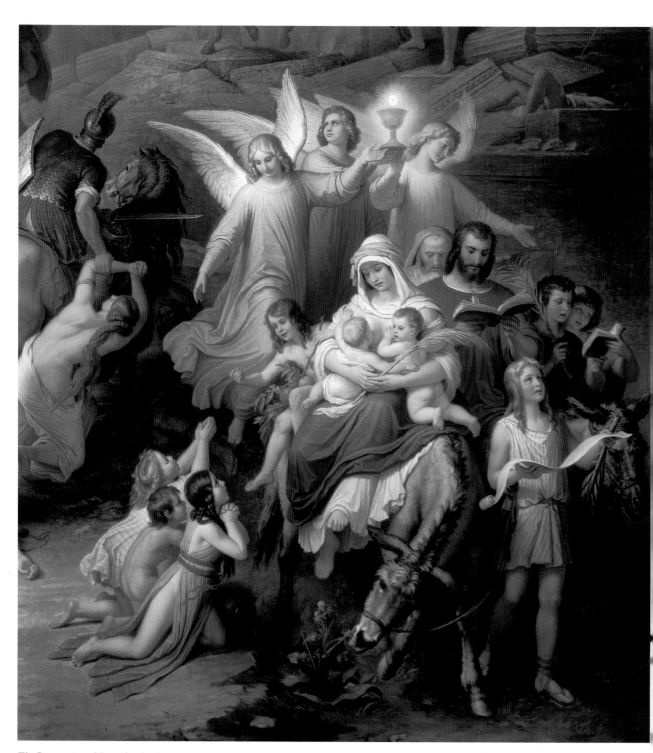

The Destruction of Jerusalem by the
Emperor Titus (detail)

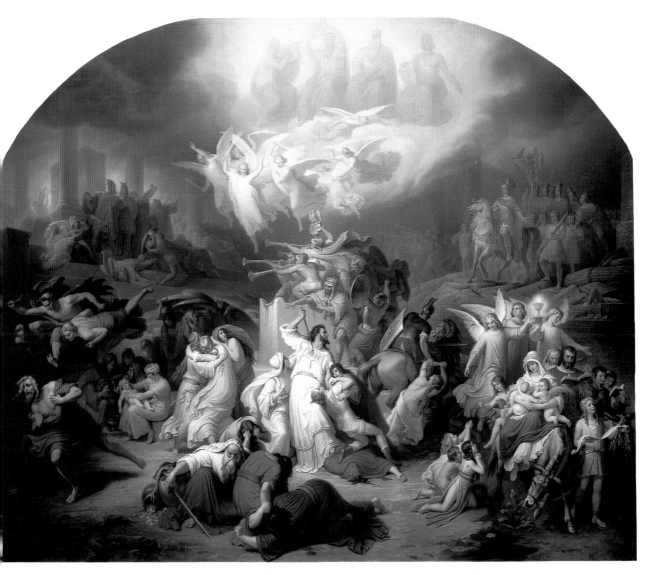

Wilhelm von Kaulbach
Arolsen 1804 – 1874 Munich
The Destruction of Jerusalem by the
Emperor Titus, 1846
Canvas, 585 × 705 cm, dated
Inv. no. WAF 403. Acquired from the
artist in 1846.

Kaulbach's historical picture is full of
allegorical meaning, turning the
destruction of Jerusalem in AD 70 into
a complex religio-historical event, its
anti-Semitic content strongly in evi-
dence. In his own opinion, the artist

was depicting a 'judgement which God
intended and carried out', as he puts it
in his detailed printed commentary on
the picture. The picture includes,
above, the great Prophets and the
seven Angels; in the right background,
the Emperor Titus and his troops; in
the middle foreground, the High Priest
taking his own life; in the left foreground, the Eternal Jew pursued by
demons; and on the opposite side, in
contrast to the Jews, a group of Chris-
tians (embodying the Nazarenes' ideal

of beauty) who escape destruction.
Ludwig I, who stipulated the dimen-
sions of this enormous painting, considered it the most important picture
in the former Neue Pinakothek. As a
key work, purchased for the exceptional sum of 35,000 guilders, it partly
determined the design of the building
and the layout of the collection.
Thanks to Kaulbach's commentary
and graphic reproductions the picture
became widely known in his lifetime.

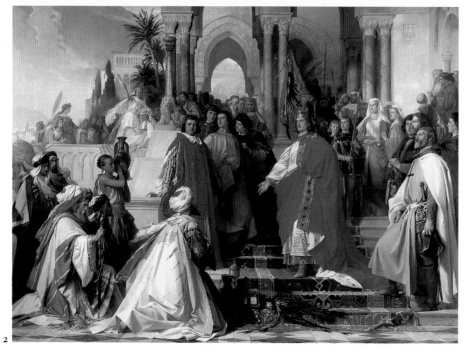

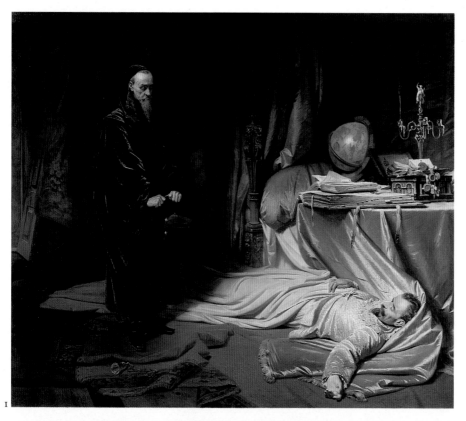

1
Karl Theodor von Piloty
Munich 1826 – 1886 Ambach
Seni before the body of Wallenstein,
1855
Canvas, 312 × 364.5 cm
Inv. no. WAF 770. Acquired from the
artist by Ludwig I in 1855.
The subject matter is taken from
Schiller's *Wallenstein*, in particular
Wallenstein's death (Act V, Scene 10,
though the action happens off-stage).
However, the artist combined several
incidents into a powerful picture successfully suggesting the approaching
disaster, which the astrologer has read
in the stars.
The painting established Piloty's reputation. From then on, he became one
of the most celebrated European historical painters of his time.

2
**Arthur Georg Freiherr von
Ramberg**
Vienna 1819 – 1875 Munich
*The court of Emperor Frederick II at
Palermo,* 1860–66, signed and dated
(1865)
Canvas, 383 × 520 cm
Inv. no. L.1777. On loan from the
Maximilianeums-Stiftung, Munich.
This painting depicts the Emperor
Frederick II Hohenstaufen in 1230,
receiving an Arab ambassador at his
court. The picture was one of a cycle
of historical paintings for the Maxi-
milianeum.

3
Karl Theodor von Piloty
Munich 1826 – 1886 Ambach
Thusnelda led in Germanicus's Triumph,
1869-73, signed
Canvas, 490 × 710 cm
Inv. no. WAF 771. Acquired from the
artist in 1874.
The subject matter comes from the
Annals of Tacitus and from Strabo,
reporting the campaigns of the
Romans in Germany in the early first
century AD. Thusnelda, wife of the
German leader Arminius and daughter
of the pro-Roman chieftain Segestes,
had been betrayed by her father and
handed over to the Romans. With her
son, Thumelicus, she was one of the
prisoners in the triumph Germanicus
held in Rome in AD 17. In the picture,
on the tribune sits the emperor
Tiberius, with Segestes on his right.
Germanicus is in front of the trium-
phal arch.
Like his German contemporaries, the
artist saw the story in its wider impli-
cations as a confrontation between
things German and things Roman, a
confrontation which at the time of the
Franco-Prussian War had assumed
special relevance.

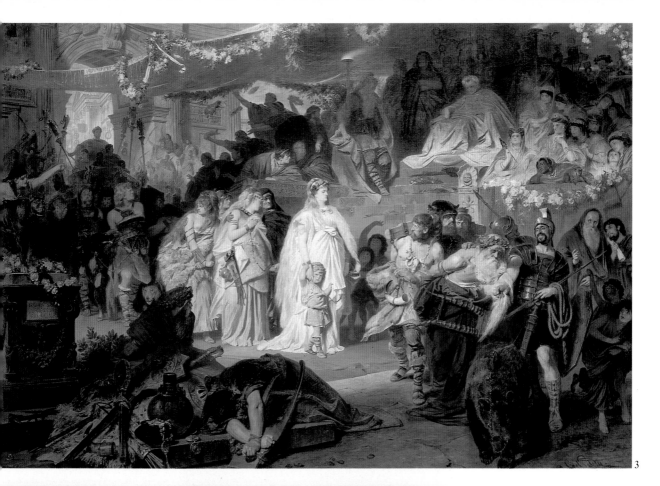

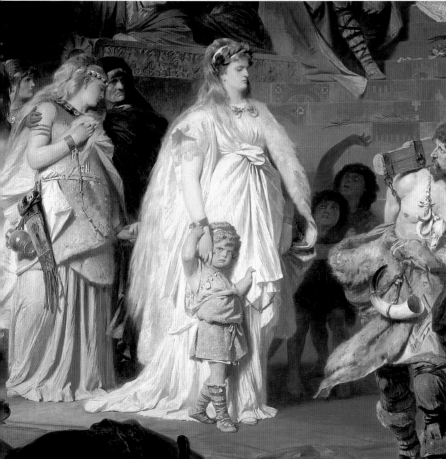

Thusnelda led in Germanicus's Triumph (detail)

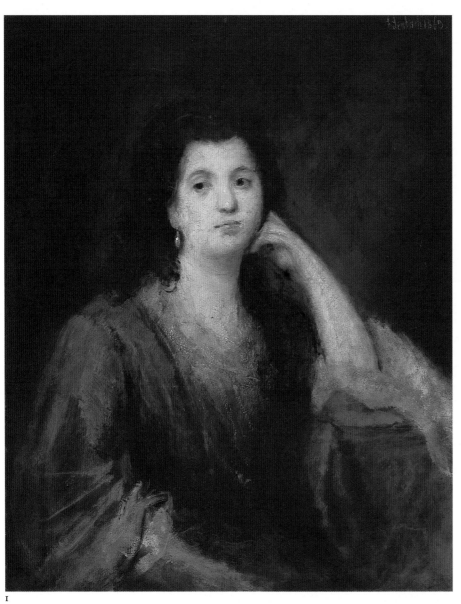

1

1

Franz von Lenbach
Schrobenhausen 1836 –
1904 Munich
A Russian princess, 1863, signed and
dated
Canvas, 83.3 × 67.4 cm
Inv. no. 8873. Acquired in 1916 from
the Heinemann Gallery, Munich.
The subject may be Maria
Nikolayevna, Countess Stroganov
(born 1819), Grand Duchess of Russia
by birth, and Dowager Duchess of
Leuchtenberg.

2

Franz von Defregger
Stronach 1835 – 1921 Munich
The latest conscripts, 1872, signed and
dated
Canvas, 53.4 × 70.2 cm
Inv. no. 9030. Acquired 1921 from the
artist's estate.
This sketch for a painting executed in
1874 (now in Vienna) depicts the last
phase, in 1809, of the Tyrolean War of
Independence against French occupa-
tion. A second, very similar sketch is
also in the Bavarian State art collections.

3

Albert von Keller
Gais 1844 – 1920 Munich
Chopin, 1873, signed and dated
Panel, 85 × 69 cm
Inv. no. 8366. Gift of the art dealer
August Humpelmayr in 1905.
Keller was especially fond of music,
which frequently inspired his work:
'Visual ideas spontaneously spring
from acoustic stimuli'. This painting
established the artist's reputation.

4

Hans Makart
Salzburg 1840 – 1884 Vienna
*The falconer, c*1880, signed
Canvas, 106.3 × 79.9 cm
Inv. no. 13291. Transferred from State
ownership in 1962

74

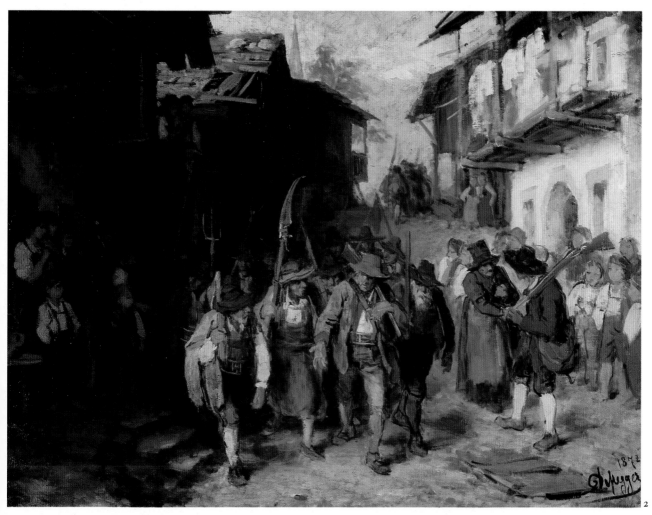

2

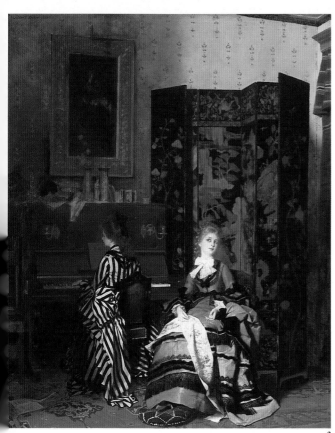

3

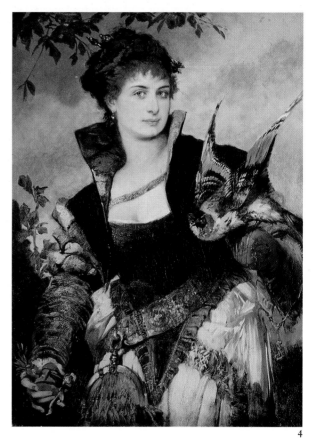

4

Hans von Marées

Like several other progressive artists of the second half of the nineteenth century –
Cézanne, for instance, or Van Gogh – Hans von Marées received little or no recognition for
most of his career. Early on, it is true, he achieved a degree of popularity and patronage for
his portraits and his pictures of horses, but for the figures he began painting from 1863 he
met with virtually none. He was dissatisfied with both of the two prevailing standards –
both with the 'official' 'history painting' and society pictures of Piloty, Keller and Lenbach,
and with the 'truth to nature' school which at last was gaining acceptance as 'contemporary
art'. Ironically Marées had points in common with both, since from the former he derived
his elevated subjects (but found the way in which they were treated artificial), and from the
Barbizon School and the 'moderns' he took a commitment to realism, while deploring the
poverty of their subject matter.

In the early 1860s, while still living in Munich, Marées turned back to the Old Masters –
at first to Rembrandt (chiefly his portraits), then to Titian, Raphael and Rubens, and finally
to classical art. After finally settling in Rome in 1875 he devoted himself increasingly to
large-scale figure compositions representing Greek mythological subjects, biblical stories or
subjects entirely of his own invention, in which he portrayed human beings simply as they
were, stripped of all transient and circumstantial appurtenances, figures to be read both as
solitaries, couples or families and as Parting, Courtship, Love, Struggle, Death. Although
he deliberately re-affirmed (notably in his use of a sombre palette) his connexion with the
Western artistic tradition, the way in which Marées created timeless symbols or allegories of
human life, and the technique in which he painted them, were entirely modern, and after
his death Marées had an enormous influence on German artists.

The Gallery's very considerable holdings of Marées's work come with few exceptions
from the Conrad Fiedler Gift of 1891. Fiedler had magnanimously extended financial support to Marées from 1868 until the artist's death.

Adolf von Hildebrand
Marburg 1847 – 1921 Munich
Conrad Fiedler, 1874-75
Marble, 44 cm high
Inv. no. B.295. Acquired in 1952 from
Werner Teupser.
Conrad Adolf Fiedler (1841-95) had a
legal training, but because of his considerable fortune did not need regular
employment. He was friendly with a
number of artists, including Adolf von
Hildebrand, Anselm Feuerbach and
Hans von Marées. He gave generous
financial support to Marées. In 1891,
he gave many works by the artist to
the Bavarian State art collections, and
these are now in the Neue Pinakothek.
Fiedler was also an important art
theorist. His writings include *On
Assessing Works of Visual Art*, 1876,
and *On Modern Naturalism and Artistic Truth*, 1881.

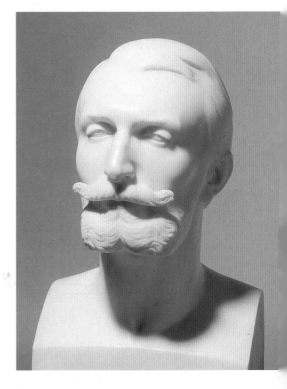

Hans von Marées
Elberfeld (Wuppertal) 1837 –
1887 Rome
The artist and Franz von Lenbach, 1863
Canvas, 54.3 × 62 cm
Inv. no. 7874. Gift of Conrad Fiedler
in 1892.
Shortly after Marées came to Munich
in 1857, he met Franz von Lenbach
(1836-1904), who later helped him
secure a commission from Adolf
Friedrich, Baron von Schack, to copy
works of the Old Masters in Italy. In
1878, Marées recalled of his years in
Munich: '. . . In those days that artistic dancing-bear was not without
influence on my life.' In this painting,
Lenbach is in the foreground, with
Marées behind him.

2

Hans von Marées
Elberfeld (Wuppertal) 1837 –
1887 Rome
Diana's rest, 1863
Canvas, 96.2 × 136 cm
Inv. no. 7866. Gift of Conrad Fiedler
in 1891.
From earliest times, Diana was identi-
fied with the Greek goddess Artemis;
she was the virgin goddess of plants,
game and hunting; she was also the
protectress of women, and in art she is
often depicted with a female retinue.
In this painting – particularly in its
colours – Marées was inspired by
Venetian painters, especially Titian,
although he had yet to visit Italy.

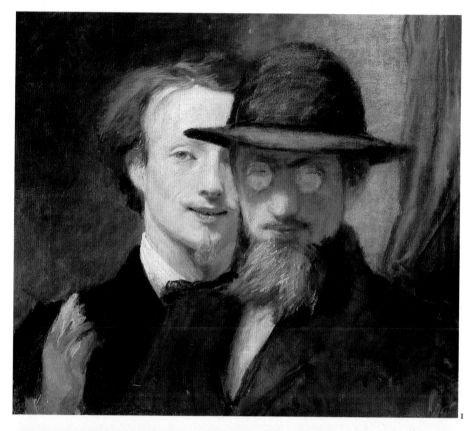

1

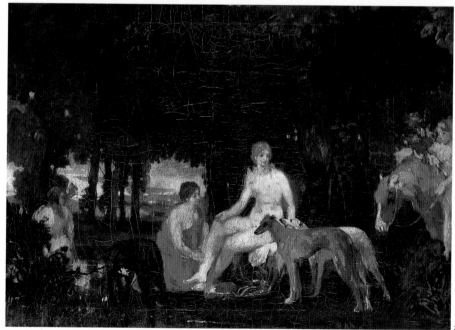

2

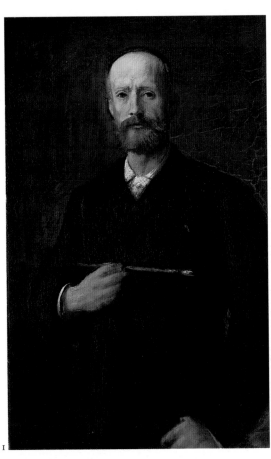

1

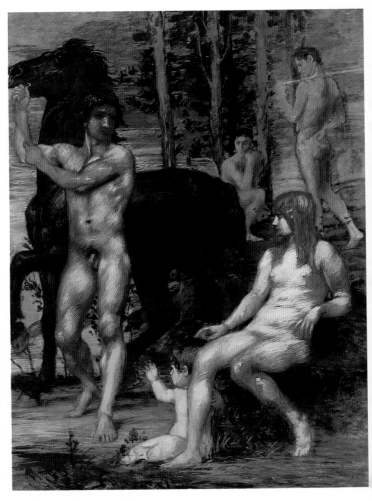

2

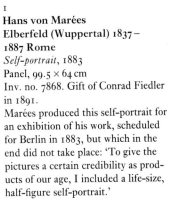

1
Hans von Marées
Elberfeld (Wuppertal) 1837 –
1887 Rome
Self-portrait, 1883
Panel, 99.5 × 64 cm
Inv. no. 7868. Gift of Conrad Fiedler
in 1891.
Marées produced this self-portrait for
an exhibition of his work, scheduled
for Berlin in 1883, but which in the
end did not take place: 'To give the
pictures a certain credibility as products of our age, I included a life-size,
half-figure self-portrait.'

2
Hans von Marées
Elberfeld (Wuppertal) 1837 –
1887 Rome
Horsetamer and nymph, 1882-83
Panel, 188.5 × 144.5 cm
Inv. no. 7862. Gift of Conrad Fiedler
in 1891.
The picture is unfinished and reveals
in many places Marées's characteristic
use of tempera, which he generally, if
not invariably, employed in the under-
painting.

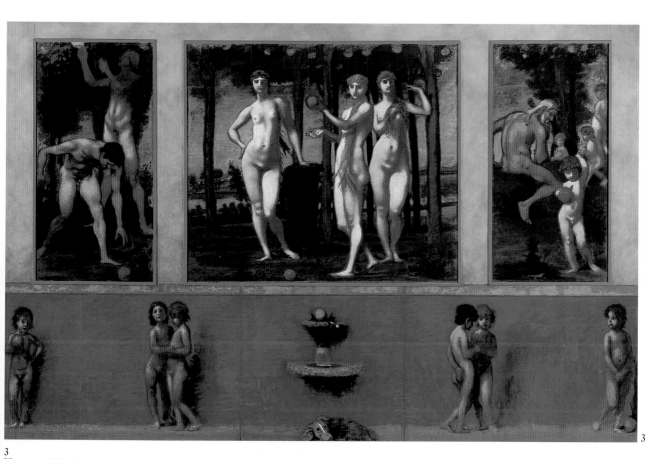

3

3
Hans von Marées
Elberfeld (Wuppertal) 1837 –
1887 Rome
The Hesperides, 1884-85
Triptych of wooden panels; middle
panel 175.5 × 205 cm; each wing
175 × 88.5 cm
Inv. no. 7854. Gift of Conrad Fiedler
in 1891.
According to ancient mythology, the
Hesperides were nymphs who had in
their care the golden apples and fruit-
trees in the divine Garden beyond the
River Ocean. A tree with golden fruit
is a symbol either of eternal youth or
of love and fertility. Accordingly,
Marées gave the Hesperides a central
position in his picture of life's cycle.

Hans von Marées
Elberfeld (Wuppertal) 1837 –
1887 Rome
St George, 1885-87
Right wing of the triptych *The Three Knights*, representing *St Hubert* in the centre and *St Martin* on the left wing
Canvas, 183 × 117 cm
Inv. no. 7858. Gift of Conrad Fiedler in 1891.
This triptych, which included a painted pedestal depicting putti, is the second version on this theme, which Marées first painted from 1880-81; of this version only the right-hand panel has survived.

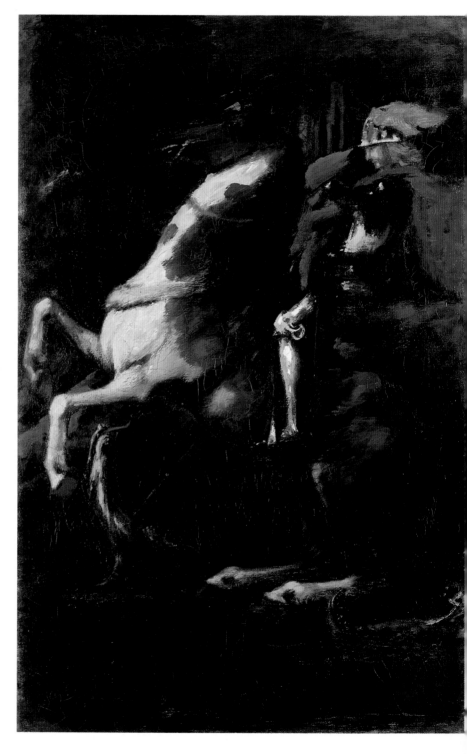

Böcklin, Feuerbach and Thoma

At a time when the work of French artists was increasing in influence, first with the landscapes of the Barbizon School, Corot, Courbet, Théodore Rousseau and others, and then with the early Impressionism of Manet, Monet and Renoir, certain German painters, including Marées, Arnold Böcklin and Anselm Feuerbach, were drawn instead to Italy. They found in Italian life, and in its countryside, art and culture, a more satisfying world than their own modern one: Italy evoked for them antiquity, which was both their inspiration and in large degree the source of their subject matter.

Marées, Feuerbach and Böcklin were, however, temperamentally very different. Böcklin was nature-loving and his art is always sensuous, while Feuerbach's pictures are more introspective and intellectual: his *Medea*, for example, is an ambitious and monumental statement, but lacks the human immediacy of Böcklin's *Pan amongst the reeds*, which engages not only the viewer's mind but also his empathy. For Böcklin *Stimmung*, or mood, was all-important, the figures bringing out the mood of the landscape and the landscape reflecting the feelings of the figures. In his earlier work, including *Pan amongst the reeds*, the *Stimmung* is less insistent; later he intensified it by every possible means, as in his burlesque *Play of the waves*. *Play of the waves* is typical of Böcklin, and far removed from Feuerbach, in its humour and in its palpable eroticism. Böcklin much more frequently than Feuerbach invented his own subject matter, even though both drew heavily on the Bible and on mythology. Several such subjects of his own devising were significant examples of a widespread new trend of the last quarter of the nineteenth century, a trend for imagery redolent with an open-ended symbolic meaning that is never declared or given context, or that may even be disturbingly enigmatic. Paintings such as *Villa by the sea* in the Gallery of about 1860, of which there are also other versions, or the several versions of *The Island of the Dead*, were of crucial importance for De Chirico and the Surrealists, while tendencies to surface decoration and a tender yearning in others, such as the *Ideal spring landscape* of 1871 (in the Schack Gallery), anticipated Art Nouveau.

Hans Thoma, twelve years the junior of his friend Böcklin, came to Italy after studying with the landscape painter Johann Wilhelm Schirmer, and there came to know Marées also. His *Memory of Orte* in the Gallery, of 1887, is typical of his attitude to Italy. Thoma was otherwise influenced by Courbet and by the Leibl circle, as can be seen in his closely observed *Landscape on the River Main*, 1875, and his *Taunus landscape* of 1890. In this last, the wanderer resting and gazing into the distance is a motif obviously derived from earlier Romantic painters such as Schwind and Friedrich.

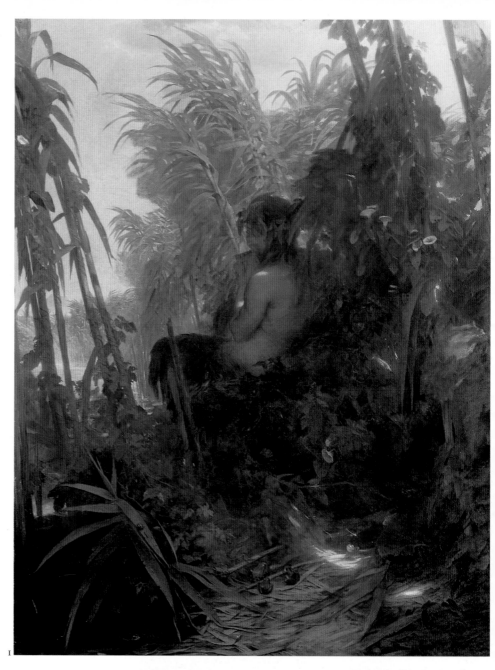

1

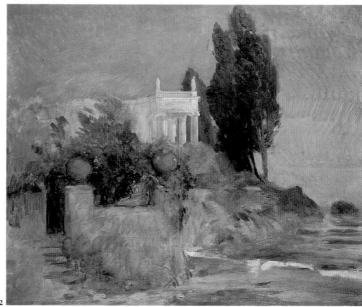

2

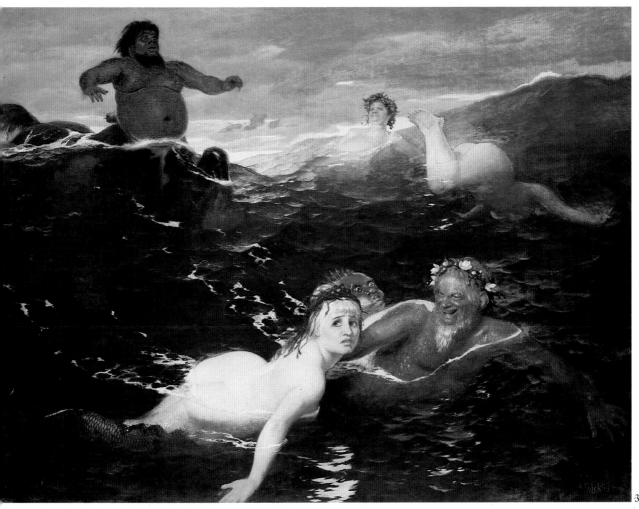

3

Arnold Böcklin
Basel 1827 – 1901 Fiesole
Pan amongst the reeds, 1859
Canvas, 199.7 × 152.6 cm
Inv. no. WAF 67. Acquired in 1859 by
Ludwig I.
Pan, the Greek god of flocks and
woods, is shown according to Ovid
Metamorphoses I, 698f). He tried to
rape the nymph Syrinx, but she was
able to transform herself into reeds
before he could do so. Pan made the
reeds into pipes (pan pipes). Böcklin
shows Pan playing a lament on them
for the vanished Syrinx. Ludwig I
purchased the picture immediately it
was completed, thereby establishing
the artist's reputation.

2
Arnold Böcklin
Basel 1827 – 1901 Fiesole
Villa by the sea, 1863
Canvas, 62 × 74 cm
Inv. no. 10811. Acquired in 1951 from
a private collection.
This sketch is probably the earliest
'state' of a picture which is known in
several versions. Adolf Friedrich,
Baron von Schack, probably saw this
small-scale picture in Böcklin's Rome
studio and then commissioned the first
large-scale version for his collection
(Schack Gallery, Munich).

3
Arnold Böcklin
Basel 1927 – 1901 Fiesole
In the play of the waves, 1883, signed
Canvas, 180.3 × 237.5 cm
Inv. no. 7754. Gift of Jan Baron
Wendelstadt of Schloss Neubeuern.
This picture is based on impressions of
the family of marine zoologist Anton
Dohrn bathing together in the Gulf of
Naples. Böcklin introduced a mytho-
logical dimension and transformed the
reality into a humorous narrative.

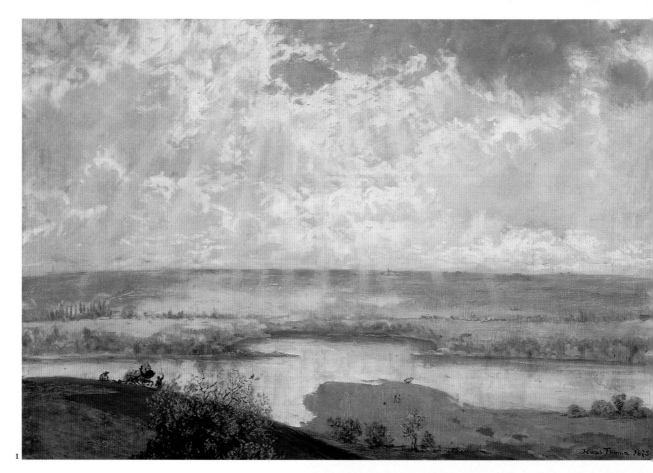

1

1
Hans Thoma
Bernau 1839 – 1924 Karlsruhe
Landscape on the River Main, 1875,
signed and dated
Canvas, 85.5 × 124.5 cm
Inv. no. 8878. Acquired in 1916 on the
Munich art market

2
Hans Thoma
Bernau 1839 – 1924 Karlsruhe
Taunus landscape, 1890, signed and
dated
Canvas, 113.3 × 88.8 cm
Inv. no. 7834. Acquired in 1891 at the
annual exhibition in the Glaspalast,
Munich

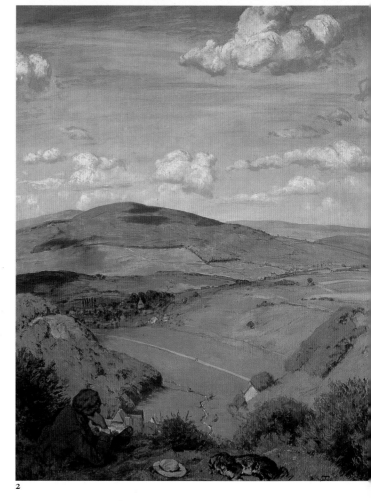

2

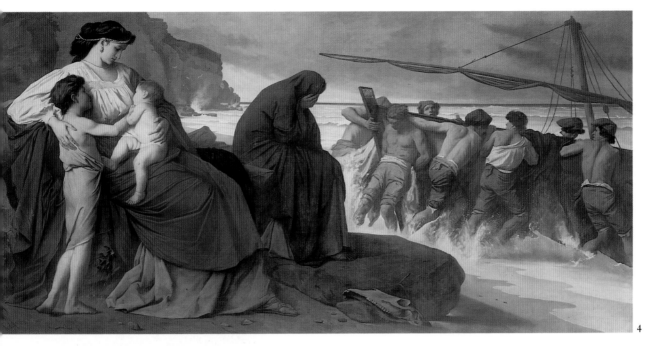

4

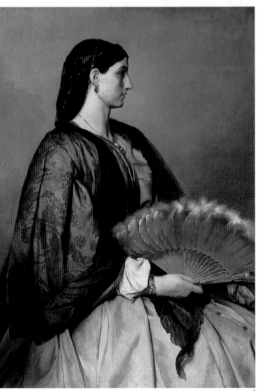

3
Anselm Feuerbach
Speyer 1829 – 1880 Venice
Nanna, 1861, signed
Canvas, 137.8 × 99.3 cm
Inv. no. 9610. Acquired in 1930 on the
Munich art market.
In 1860, Feuerbach became interested
in Nanna Risi, a working-class Roman
who reminded him of Raphael's
Madonnas. The same year Nanna left
her husband and children to live with
the artist, staying with him for five
years. During this time, the artist
executed several portraits of her and
used her as a model for several of his
historical figures.

4
Anselm Feuerbach
Speyer 1829 – 1880 Venice
Medea, 1870, signed and dated
Canvas, 197 × 395 cm
Inv. no. 9826. Acquired by Ludwig II;
in State ownership since 1932.
The sorceress Medea, daughter of
King Aietes of Colchis, helped Jason
of the Argonauts in his quest for the
Golden Fleece. She had two sons by
Jason, whom she murdered when he
left her. A performance of Ernest
Legouvé's play *Medea* in Rome in
1866, with Adelaide Ristori in the title
rôle, excited Feuerbach's obsession
with the subject, which he painted
several times.

Wilhelm Leibl and his circle

Even while he was studying at the Munich Akademie, from 1864 to 1869, Wilhelm Leibl was the dominant personality of a circle of artists, of whom the original nucleus were Johann Sperl, Theodor Alt, Rudolf Hirth du Frênes and Fritz Schider. They were joined in the early 1870s by Wilhelm Trübner, Carl Schuch and several others. Leibl and his friends were committed to the principle of 'truth to nature'. Particularly Leibl and Schuch favoured as subjects figures, landscapes, domestic scenes and still lifes, which they portrayed faithfully but not unimaginatively according to their direct experience. They found stimulus and support from artists in Munich outside the Akademie of an earlier generation, such as Schleich, Lier and Langko, who had had contacts with artists of the Barbizon School. They also drew inspiration from seventeenth-century Dutch landscape and genre painting, and from a tradition of admiration for such art that had been growing since Georges Michel had revived French interest in it in the early nineteenth century. As ordinary citizens' art, it conformed well with their ideal. For the Leibl circle, the Dutch were 'modern', and in his 1869 portrait of *Frau Gedon* Leibl borrowed quite obviously from Rembrandt's *Jan Six*. His picture aroused considerable attention at the Internationale Kunstausstellung (International Art Exhibition) in Munich of that year, bringing Leibl the friendship of Courbet and an invitation to Paris, where the young German was no less successful.

Courbet and the Barbizon School were also directly influential on these artists. In *Kähnsdorf Lock* Schuch clearly depends on a similar motif in Courbet, and in his late landscapes time and again develops ideas to be found in the French painter. Further developments in French art also had their impact, and Manet's influence is apparent not only in Leibl's portrait of *Lina Kirchdorffer*, completed shortly after his return from Paris, but also later in still lifes by Schuch, who lived in Paris from 1882 to 1894.

Other artists in the circle were less rigorous in their adherence to truth to experience: Sperl, for instance, had a penchant for the sentimental and anecdotal and never eliminated it from his work, while Trübner's later output was generally uninspired, though his *Studio scene* of 1872 is one of the finest pictures produced by the Leibl circle.

Leibl and his friends received no greater recognition in their lifetimes than the appreciation of a small circle of other artists and connoisseurs. While Lenbach was celebrated throughout Europe and could build himself a villa in Munich in an Italian Renaissance style, Leibl, disgusted by the art market, moved out to the country in 1873.

Wilhelm Leibl
Cologne 1844–1900 Würzburg
Mina Gedon, 1868–69
Canvas, 119.5 × 95.7 cm
Inv. no. 8708. Acquired in 1913 on the Munich art market.
Mina Gedon, the young wife of the Munich architect, Lorenz Gedon, did many tiring sittings for Leibl whilst pregnant. Leibl scored great success at exhibitions in Munich and Paris in 1869–70 with her portrait. Artists especially, including Gustave Courbet, were enthusiastic about the painting.

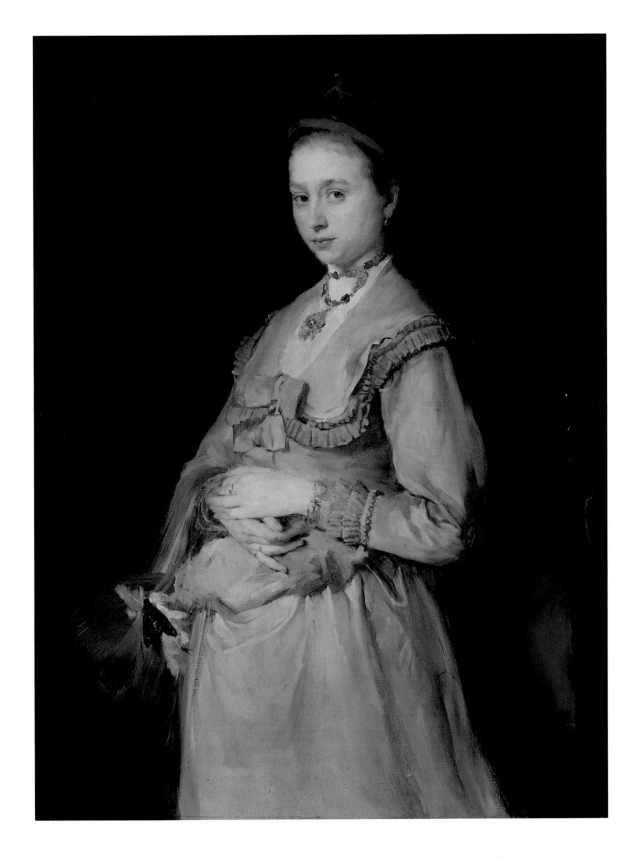

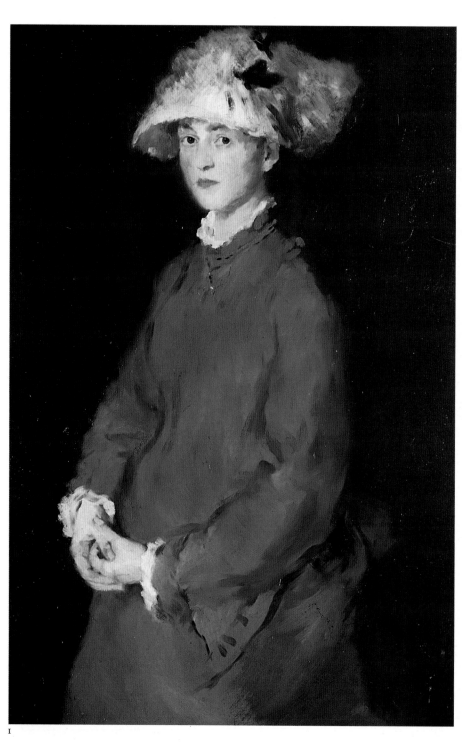

1

1
Wilhelm Leibl
Cologne 1844–1900 Würzburg
Lina Kirchdorffer, 1871
Canvas, 111 × 83.5 cm
Inv. no. 8446. Acquired in 1907 on the
Munich art market.
Leibl produced this picture of his
niece Lina immediately after his return
from Paris. In the fluid, sensitive
brushwork, he shows the influence of
Edouard Manet. Lina married the
painter Fritz Schider in 1873.

2
Wilhelm Leibl
Cologne 1844-1900 Würzburg
The painter Jean Paul Selinger, c1880,
signed
Canvas, 45 × 37 cm
Inv. no. 8264. Acquired in 1903 on the
Munich art market.
Selinger (1850-1909), came to Munich
in the mid-1870s and there, with
fellow Americans Frank Duveneck,
William Merrit Chase and J. Frank
Currier, he joined Wilhelm Leibl's
circle. He returned to the USA in
1881, to settle in Providence, Rhode
Island.

3
Rudolf Hirth du Frênes
Gräfentonna 1846 –
1916 Miltenberg
Carl Schuch, 1874, signed and dated
Canvas, 69 × 50.3 cm
Inv. no. 7835. Acquired in 1891 at the
annual exhibition in the Glaspalast,
Munich.
Carl Eduard Schuch (Vienna 1846-
1903) was a student from 1865 to 1869
at the Vienna Academy, mainly under
Halauska. He then went to Italy, and
from there to Munich where he
became a friend notably of Wilhelm
Trübner and Wilhelm Leibl, who both
had a vital influence on him. In 1876,
Schuch, who had until then mainly
painted landscapes, began an extensive
series of still lifes, and moved to
Venice. From there he went to Paris in
1882. During the summer of 1886, he
painted landscapes at Saut du Doubs,
which show the growing influence of
Courbet. In the still lifes of this period
he also responded to the work of
French painters, including Edouard
Manet. In 1894, mental illness forced
the artist to return to Vienna, where
from 1898 onwards he lived in a psy-
chiatric institution.

4
Wilhelm Trübner
Heidelberg 1851 – 1917 Karlsruhe
In the studio, 1872, signed and dated
Canvas, 82 × 61 cm.
Inv. no. 8108. Acquired in 1899 from
the artist

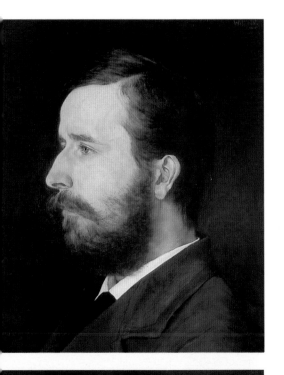

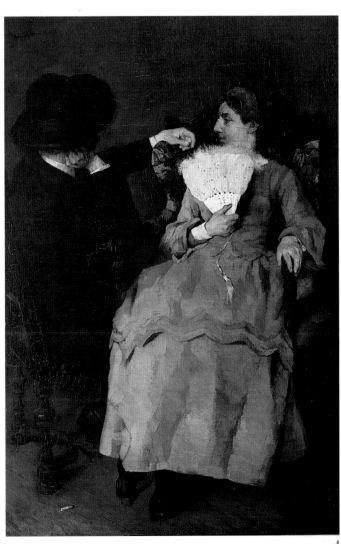

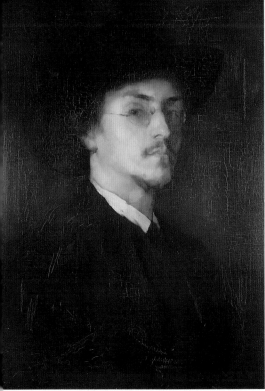

4

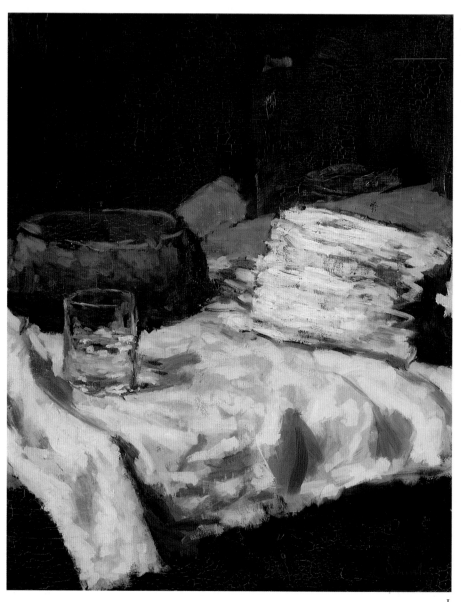

I

1

Carl Schuch
Vienna 1846–1903 Vienna
*Still life with asparagus, c*1885-90,
signed with a facsimile stamp
Canvas, 79 × 63 cm
Inv. no. 8907. Acquired in 1916 at the
auction of the Schmeil collection in
Berlin

2

Carl Schuch
Vienna 1846–1903 Vienna
*Still life with apples, wine glass and tin
jug, c*1876, signed with a facsimile
stamp
Canvas, 69.5 × 92 cm
Inv. no. 8563. Acquired in 1909 at the
Schuch retrospective held at the
Kunstverein, Munich.
This is one of the first still lifes ever
painted by Schuch. There is a very
similar version, painted the same year,
in the National Gallery, East Berlin.

3

Adolf Hölzel
Olmütz 1853–1934 Stuttgart
*Reading the Holy Book, c*1890, signed
Canvas, 40 × 32 cm
Inv. no. 7891. Acquired in 1892 on the
Berlin art market.
This picture has the detail characteris-
tic of the artist's early paintings.
Before long, he adopted a noticeably
broader and flatter style, until finally
he moved to complete abstraction.

4

Johann Sperl
Buch 1840–1914 Bad Aibling
*The Kindergarten, c*1884, signed
Canvas, 71.3 × 101.6 cm.
Inv. no. BGM 5. Acquired in 1984 for
the collection of the Bayerische
Landesbank

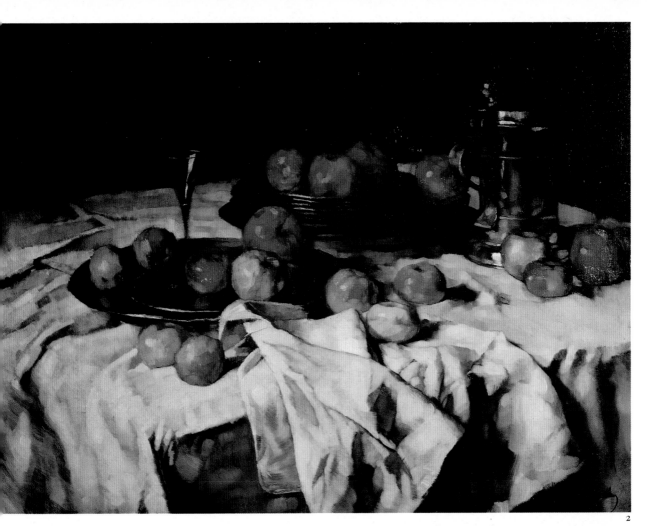

2

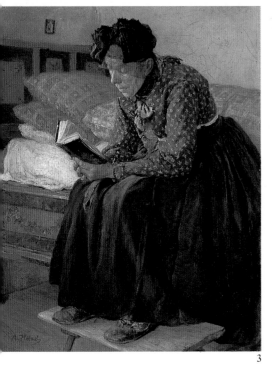

3

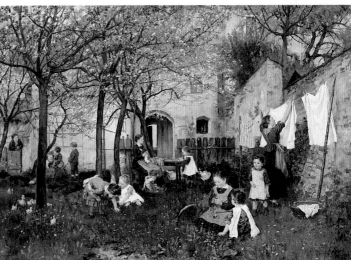

4

French Impressionism and Post-Impressionism

Impressionism means painting everyday life in the open air: the term was coined from a painting of 1872 by Monet entitled *Impression, soleil levant* (Sunrise: an impression), and was applied to the artists, including Monet, Cézanne, Degas, Pissarro, Renoir and Sisley, who participated in an exhibition at Nadar's Gallery in 1874. However, not only did these painters differ very considerably among themselves in style and approach, but also Gauguin and Van Gogh, who had very little in common with Monet, Renoir or Sisley, both had 'Impressionist' phases.

While the art recognised and promoted by the academies was still 'history painting' above all, painters of the Barbizon School and others who shared their views had turned instead to landscape and to ordinary middle-class or peasant subjects, championing 'truth to nature' or experience. This was also the guiding principle of the Impressionists, who, however, stimulated partly by Constable and by Delacroix, found it to require a lightening of the palette, the avoidance of grey and ochre for shading, and the use of unmixed, luminous colours. They were led to employ a looser, more spontaneous brushwork, with which, inevitably, they were unable to create the illusion of solidity and the distinctness of things, but achieved instead, with flat dabs on the canvas, a homogeneous surface in which all was merged in a single effect. Sketchily painted in brilliant colours, unburdened by significance, the landscapes, portraits and scenes of ordinary life that they painted from the early 1870s reflect the cheerful and carefree side both of nature and of life – even though there is a considerable difference between the work of Monet, Renoir and Sisley and that of Manet, Degas and Cézanne.

Edouard Manet, before he became an Impressionist, was the last great artist in the Western tradition with a feeling for the substance and texture of the subjects he painted – flowers, glass, fabrics or indeed people, who in his work are alive both in flesh and in spirit. Manet's human subjects have a distinct self-awareness, combining an outward elegance with a certain melancholy, that one can easily believe was characteristic of the Parisian *haute bourgeoisie* of the second half of the nineteenth century. His painting in the Gallery, *Breakfast in the studio*, 1868, is a masterpiece of this early period and one of the finest he ever produced. Though he turned to Impressionism, or to *plein-air* painting as described above, about 1873-74, Manet retained the distinctive, portrait quality of his figures, whereas for Monet, Pissarro and Renoir figures had little importance or at least minimal characterisation.

Edgar Degas had much more in common with Manet, his personal friend, than with the other Impressionists. Degas portrayed figures with a still sharper, increasingly critical eye, and with irony, sometimes even sarcasm – as in his numerous pictures of women taking baths dating from the second half of the 1880s. While the women contort their bodies in awkward poses as they wash and dry, Degas captures them from unconventional angles in compositions obviously influenced by Japanese prints.

From this point in Degas's development Henri de Toulouse-Lautrec's art begins. He is Degas taken to an extreme, and irony and wit are the dominant and vital ingredient of his prints and posters. They are much less pronounced in his early paintings, influenced by Manet, but emerge more strongly in his drawings and oil-studies of the theatre and of brothels, which commence in the second half of the 1880s.

Paul Cézanne abandoned his early sombre, intensely passionate style and subject matter to take up Impressionism under the tutelage of Camille Pissarro, though he never followed the general tendency to a free, flat and sketchy execution. In his landscapes, still lifes, portraits and figure compositions (in particular his series of *Bathers*) he gave people and things

Edouard Manet
Paris 1832 – 1883 Paris
Le Déjeuner dans l'Atelier, 1868, signed
Canvas, 118 × 154 cm
Inv. no. 8638. Given in 1911 by Georg Ernst von Schmidt-Reissig as part of the Tschudi donation.
This picture combines the genres of interior scene and portraiture. The young man is Manet's illegitimate son, Léon Leenhoff-Koell, by Suzanne Leenhoff, whom the artist subsequently married.

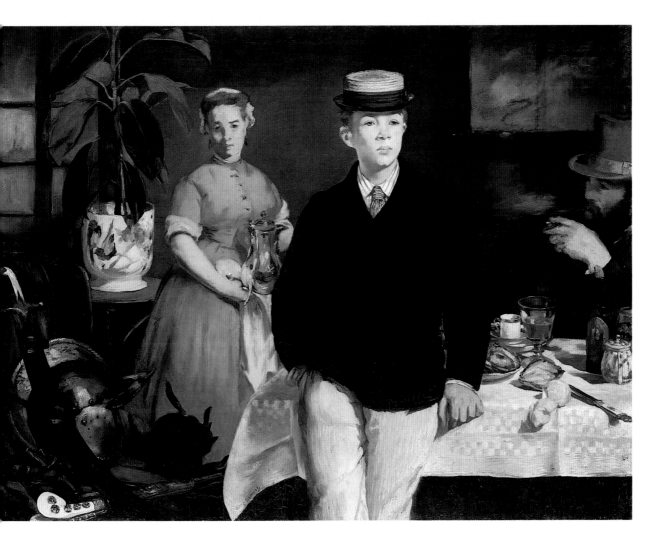

an original weight and pregnancy by removing them outside time and circumstance. With the waning of Neo-Impressionism and Art Nouveau Cézanne became a seminal influence on the new movement of Cubism.

For the emergence of Art Nouveau Paul Gauguin and his circle (Emile Bernard, Paul Sérusier and others) were the most important figures. These men were stimulated particularly by Japanese woodcuts to follow out the tendency in the Impressionist style towards two-dimensionality and decoration for its own sake. Gauguin in addition liked to embrace mystic, universal themes, combining motifs of South Sea Islands culture in a basically Christian outlook (for example, in the Gallery, *Te tamari no atua*, 1896): he is therefore also an important figure in the Symbolist trend.

Vincent van Gogh, schooled in the Old Masters, in the work of the Barbizon School and The Hague School, in Delacroix and then in Impressionism, was an individual and isolated figure. He, once again, dedicated himself to painting pictures of universal significance, encompassing all human joy and sorrow.

Nearly all the works in this section were donated between 1911 and 1913 by Munich citizens and also some artists as a memorial to Hugo von Tschudi (1851-1911, Director of the Bayerische Staatsgemäldesammlungen from 1909).

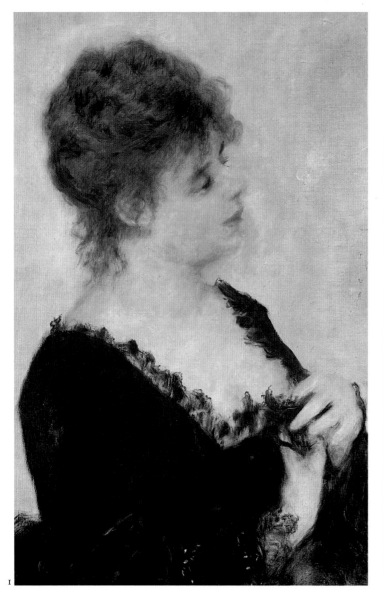

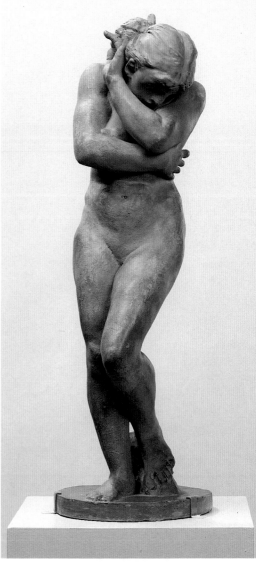

1
Auguste Renoir
Limoges 1841 – 1919 Cagnes-sur-
Mer
Young woman in a black blouse, 1876,
signed
Canvas, 60.5 × 40.5 cm
Inv. no. 8644. Given anonymously in
1912 as part of the Tschudi donation

2
Auguste Rodin
Paris 1840 – 1917 Meudon
Eve, 1885(?)
Terracotta, 72 cm high
Inv. no. B.355. Acquired in 1959 on
the art market in Switzerland.
Rodin created the figure of *Eve*,
together with that of *Adam*, for his
Gates of Hell about 1880-81, but he
did not retain the original design. A
cast 170 cm high exists from this early
stage. Around 1885, Rodin created a

marble version 70 cm high, which was
followed by ten further marble versions of *Eve*. Judging by its size, this
figure in terracotta is related to the
first marble version.

3
Edouard Manet
Paris 1832 – 1883 Paris
The boat, 1874, signed
Canvas, 82.5 × 105 cm
Inv. no. 8759. Acquired in 1914 as
part of the Tschudi donation.
This work was painted in the year of
the first Impressionist exhibition, and
shows Claude Monet with his wife in
the artist's boat, in which Monet
painted several of his pictures. That
year, Manet had a particularly close
friendship with him.

4
Claude Monet
Paris 1840 – 1926 Giverny
The bridge over the Seine at Argenteuil,
1874, signed and dated
Canvas, 60 × 81.3 cm
Inv. no. 8642. Acquired in 1912 on the
Berlin art market.
After the Franco-Prussian War, Monet
lived for five years in Argenteuil, as
did Edouard Manet and Alfred Sisley.
The bridge shown here was built in
1872.

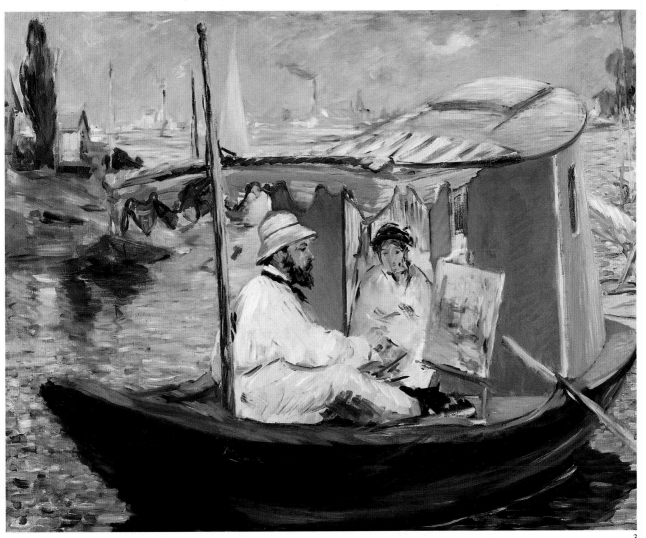

3

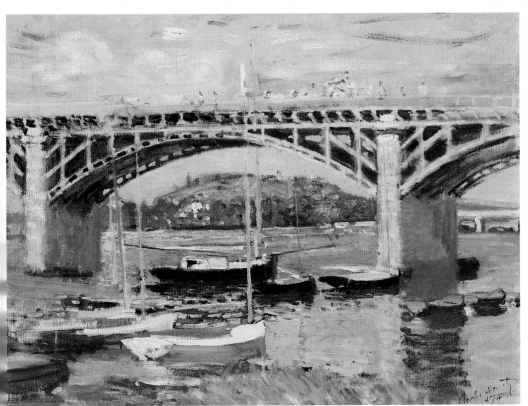

4

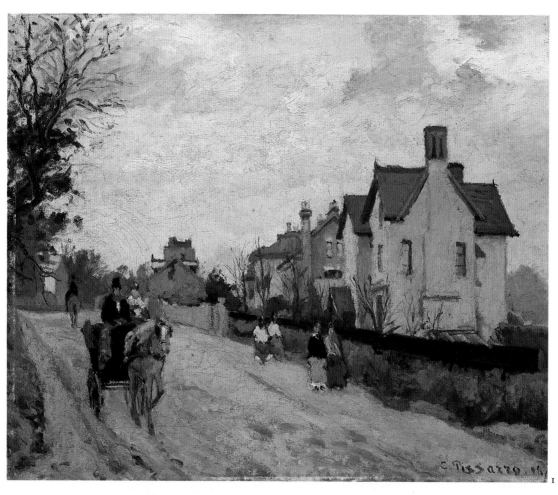

1

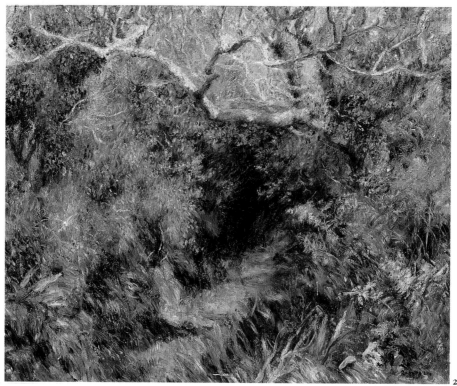

2

Camille Pissarro
St-Thomas 1830 – 1903 Paris
A road in Upper Norwood, 1871,
signed
Canvas, 45.3 × 55.5 cm
Inv. no. 8699. Given in 1913 by
L. Prager as part of the Tschudi
donation.
Like Claude Monet and Alfred Sisley,
Pissarro moved to England during the
Franco-Prussian War. Upper Nor-
wood is a southern suburb of London.

2
Auguste Renoir
Limoges 1841 – 1919 Cagnes-sur-Mer
Landscape in the South of France
c1890, signed
Canvas, 53.7 × 65.3 cm
Inv. no. 14217. Bequeathed by Elly
Koehler in 1971

3
Edgar Degas
Paris 1834 – 1917 Paris
After bathing, c1888-92, signed and
inscribed 'A M J Stchoukine'
Pastel on paper, 48 × 63 cm
Inv. no. 13136. Acquired on the
London art market in 1961.
The inscription indicates that this
pastel was a gift from the artist to the
Russian merchant and well-known col-
lector, Sergei Ivanovich Shtshukin,
who had met Degas in 1908, and
appreciated his work.

4
Edgar Degas
Paris 1834 – 1917 Paris
Henri and Alexis Rouart, 1895, signed
Canvas, 92 × 73 cm
Inv. no. 13681. Acquired in 1965 on
the New York art market.
Henri Rouart (1833-1912), a friend of
Degas, was an engineer who also
painted and even exhibited with the
Impressionists. Above all, he was one
of the most important collectors of his
time. He is depicted here with his son
Alexis. There exist preparatory draw-
ings for both subjects.

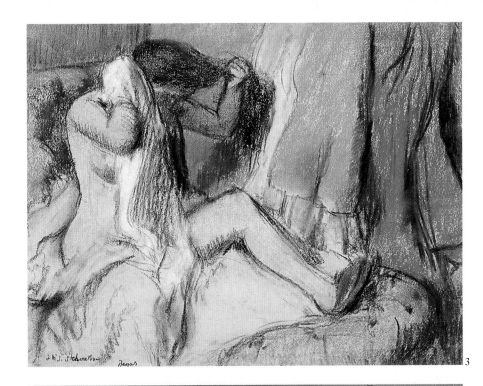
3

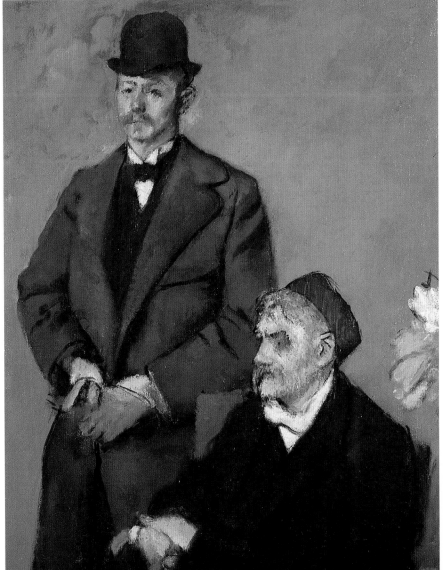
4

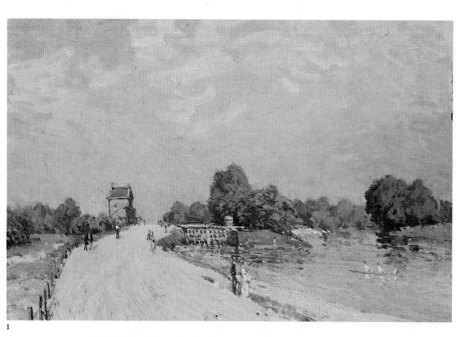

1

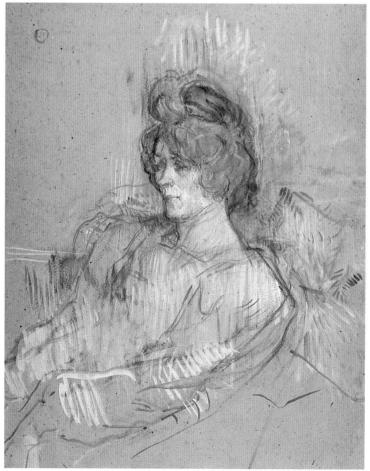

2

1
Alfred Sisley
Paris 1839 – 1899 Moret-sur-Loing
A road in Hampton Court, 1874, signed
and dated
Canvas, 38.8 × 55.8 cm
Inv. no. 13134. Acquired in 1961 on
the Paris art market.
The singer Jean-Baptiste Fauré made
it possible for Sisley to visit England
in 1874. He also collected the artist's
work.

2
Henri de Toulouse-Lautrec
Albi 1864 – 1901 Malrome
A female portrait, 1897, signed
Board, 63 × 48 cm
Inv. no. 8666. Gift of Eduard Arnhold
and Robert von Mendelssohn as part
of the Tschudi donation in 1912

3
Edgar Degas
Paris 1834 – 1917 Paris
The ironer, c1869, bearing the
executor's stamp
Canvas, 92.5 × 74 cm
Inv. no. 14310. Acquired in 1972 on
the New York art market.
The picture is unfinished. The model
was Emma Dobigny, whose portrait
Degas painted in 1869.

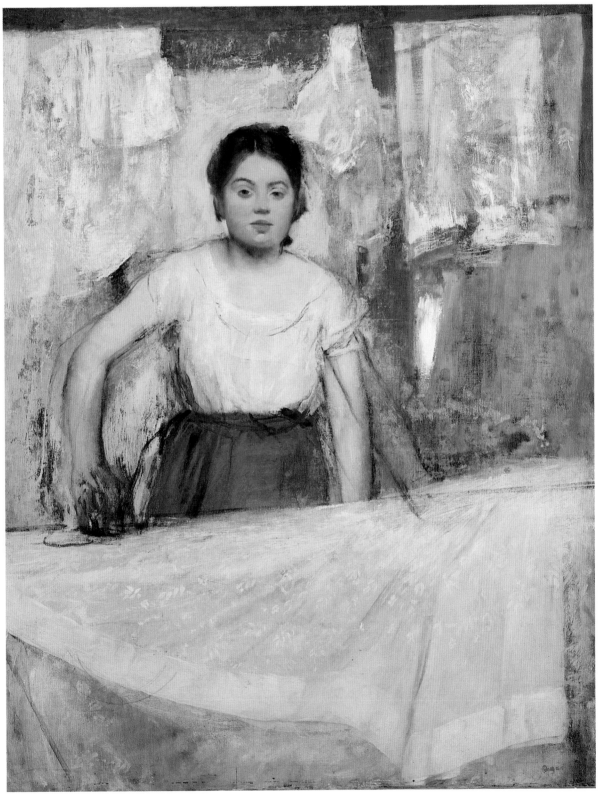

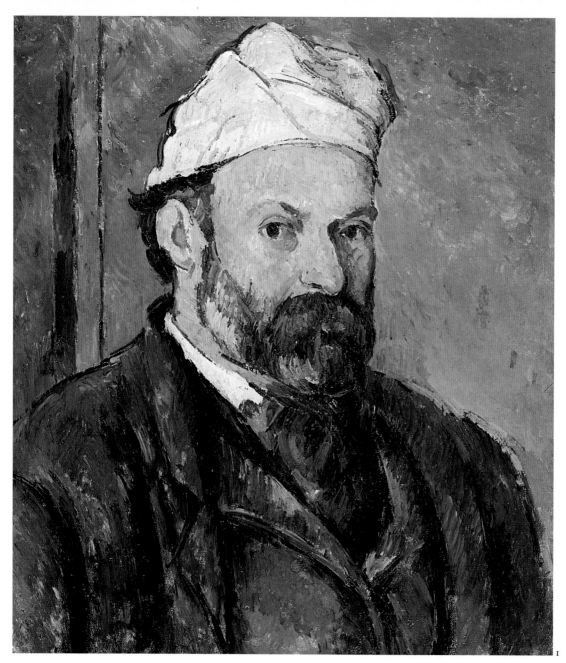

1

Paul Cézanne
Aix-en-Provence 1839 –
1906 Aix-en-Provence
*Self-portrait, c*1875-77
Canvas, 55.5 × 46 cm
Inv. no. 8648. Given in 1912 by
Eduard Arnhold and Robert von
Mendelssohn as part of the Tschudi
donation

2

Paul Cézanne
Aix-en-Provence 1839 –
1906 Aix-en-Provence
*The railway cutting, c*1870
Canvas, 80 × 129 cm
Inv. no. 8646. Acquired in 1912 as
part of the Tschudi donation.
The railway cutting was not far from
the Jas de Bouffan, near Aix-en-
Provence in the Arc valley. In the
background is Cézanne's first
depiction of Mont St-Victoire, which
was to be such a frequent motif in his
paintings in later years.

3

Paul Cézanne
Aix-en-Provence 1839 –
1906 Aix-en-Provence
*Still life, c*1885
Canvas, 73 × 92 cm
Inv. no. 8647. Acquired in 1912 as
part of the Tschudi donation

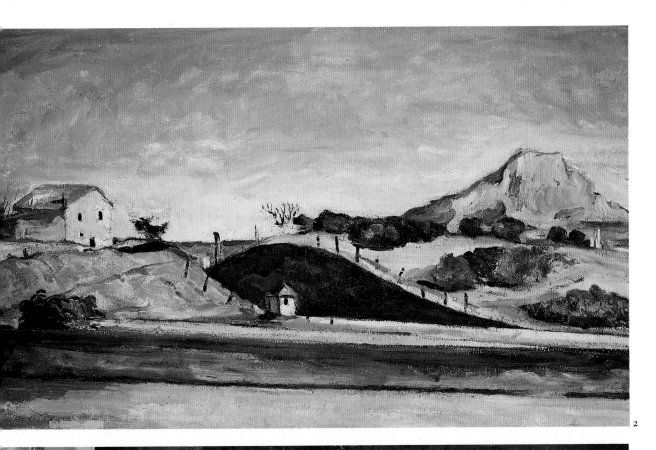

2

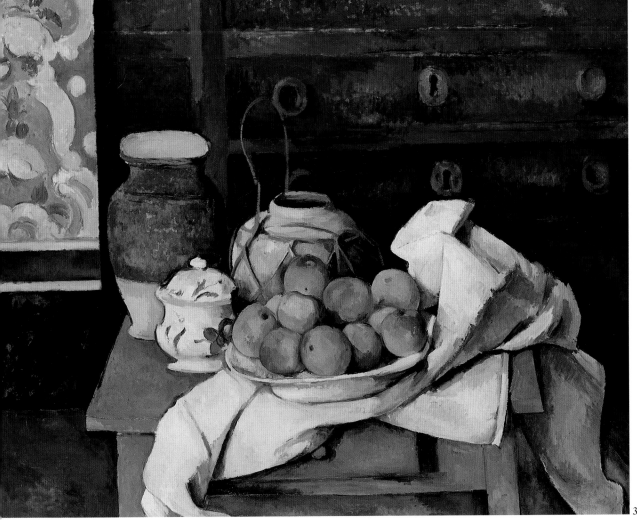

3

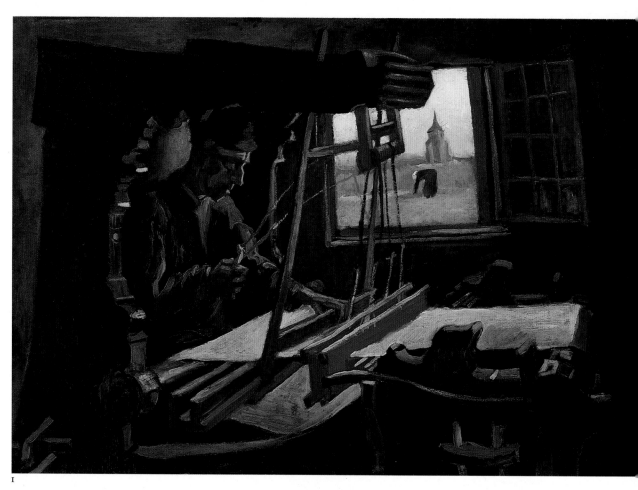

1

1
Vincent van Gogh
Groot-Zundert, 1853 –
1890 Auvers-sur-Oise
The weaver, 1884
Canvas, 67.7 × 93.2 cm
Inv. no. 14249. Bequeathed in 1971 by
Theodor und Woty Werner.
During his time in Nuenen (1883-85),
Van Gogh produced numerous draw-
ings, watercolours and oils of the
weavers he met whilst he was there.

2
Vincent van Gogh
Groot-Zundert 1853 –
1890 Auvers-sur-Oise
Vase with sunflowers, 1888, signed
Canvas, 91 × 72 cm
Inv. no. 8672. Given anonymously in
1912 as part of the Tschudi donation.
Van Gogh created this, and his other
pictures of sunflowers, to decorate his
house in Arles, and the rooms of his
friends Paul Gauguin and Emile Bernard, whose arrival he so looked for-
ward to. Van Gogh also intended the
sunflower pictures to be the side
panels of a triptych with his rocking-
chair in the centre (the painting '*La
Berceuse*').

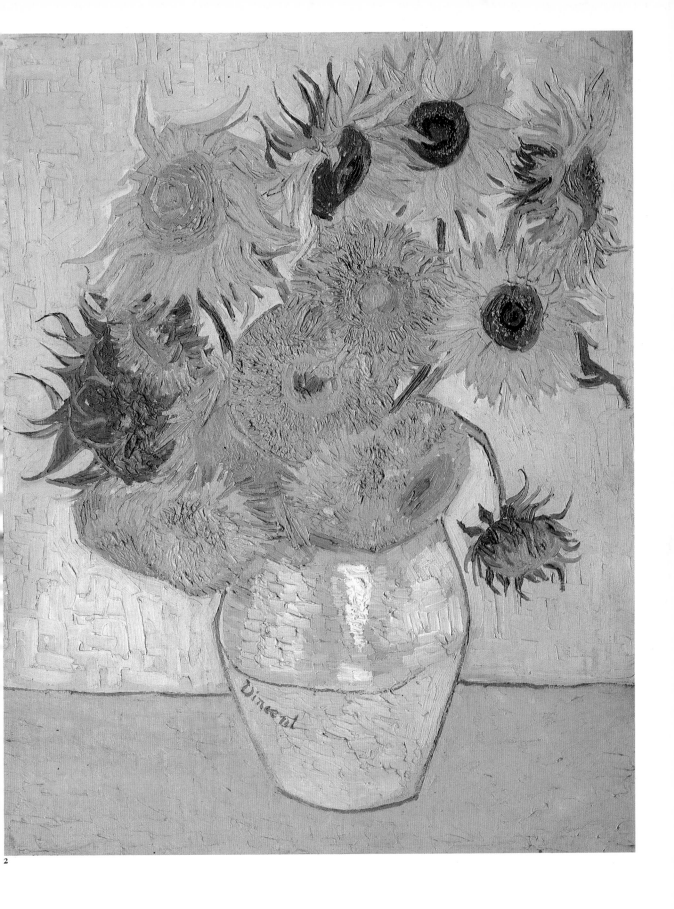

2

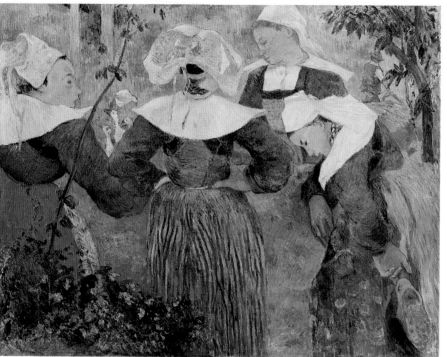

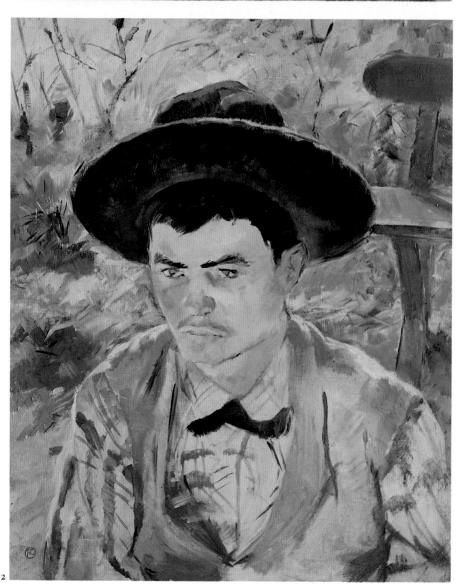

1

Paul Gauguin
Paris 1848–1903 Atuana
Four Breton women, 1886, signed and
dated
Canvas, 72 × 90 cm
Inv. no. 8701. Given in 1913 by Emy
Roth as part of the Tschudi donation

2

Henri de Toulouse-Lautrec
Albi 1864–1901 Malromé
The young Routy at Céleyran, 1882,
signed with a monogram stamp
Canvas, 61 × 49.8 cm
Inv. no. 14928. Acquired in 1984 with
the aid of the Ernst von Siemens art
fund.
Routy was a farm labourer, who
worked for the castle of Céleyran near
Narbonne. The castle belonged to
Toulouse-Lautrec's grandmother, and
the artist was a frequent visitor in his
early years. He painted the castle and
its estate from 1880 onwards; in 1882
he began a series of works devoted to
the young Routy.

3

Vincent van Gogh
Groot-Zundert 1853–
1890 Auvers-sur-Oise
The plain at Auvers, 1890
Canvas, 73.5 × 92 cm
Inv. no. 9584. Acquired in 1929 on the
Paris art market.
The artist reached Auvers on 21 May
1890. From a letter dated 23 July
which had a sketch of the picture it
can be deduced that he had just fin-
ished it.

4

Vincent van Gogh
Groot-Zundert 1853–
1890 Auvers-sur-Oise
View of Arles, 1889
Canvas, 72 × 92 cm
Inv. no. 8671. Given in 1912 by Emy
Roth as part of the Tschudi donation.
This is one of several views of Arles
which van Gogh produced after he
moved there in 1888. In contrast to
other pictures, however, the restriction
of the view by poplar trees indicates
the artist's resignation and virtual
abandonment of his hope of creating
an ideal community there. The cause
was the mental illness which necessi-
tated his confinement in the psychiat-
ric institution at St-Rémy.

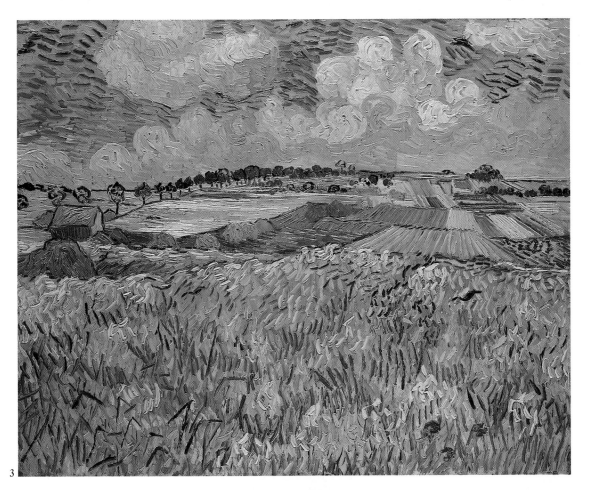

3

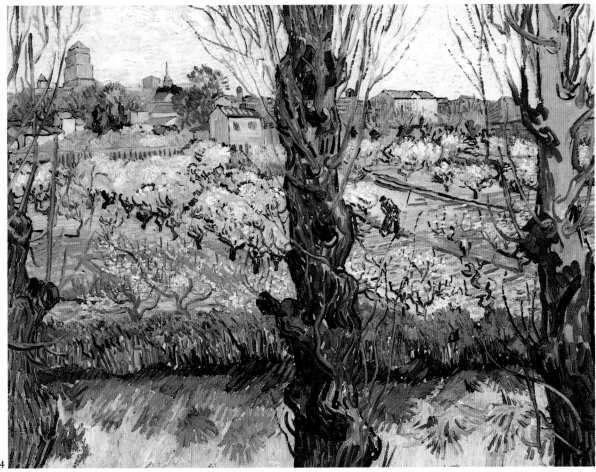

4

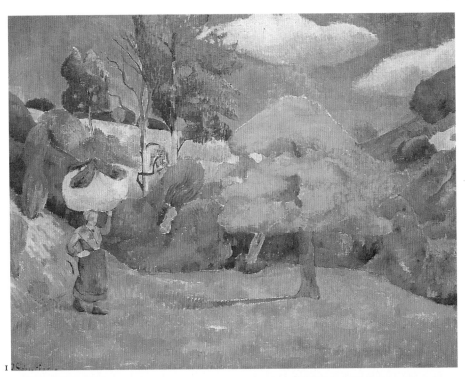

1

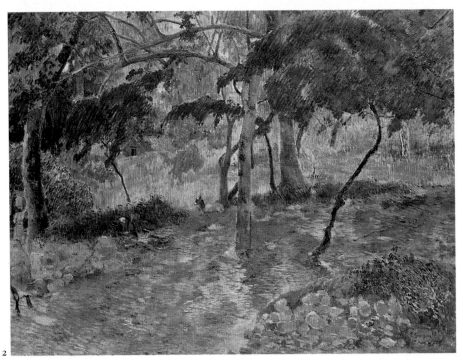

2

Paul Sérusier
Paris 1863–1927 Morlaix
Breton woman going down to the washing-place, 1890, signed and dated
Canvas, 73.7 × 93 cm
Inv. no. 12222. Bequeathed by the painter Hugo Troendle in 1955

2
Paul Gauguin
Paris 1848–1903 Atuana
Tropical landscape in Martinique, 1887, signed and dated
Canvas, 90 × 116 cm
Inv. no. 8653. Given in 1912 by Eduard Arnhold and Robert von Mendelssohn as part of the Tschudi donation.
This picture was painted in summer 1887, in Martinique, in the French Antilles.

3
Paul Gauguin
Paris 1848–1903 Atuana
The Birth of Christ, 1896, signed and dated and inscribed 'TE TAMARI NO ATUA'
Canvas, 96 × 131 cm
Inv. no. 8652. Given in 1912 by Eduard Arnhold and Robert von Mendelssohn as part of the Tschudi donation.
The inscription means 'Children of God', although the artist probably meant 'Child of God'. The picture was obviously painted to mark the birth of a child, in 1896, to the Tahitian woman, Pajura, whom Gauguin had taken as his wife. The child died a few days later. Deliberate references to Christian themes had already appeared in the artist's earlier work.

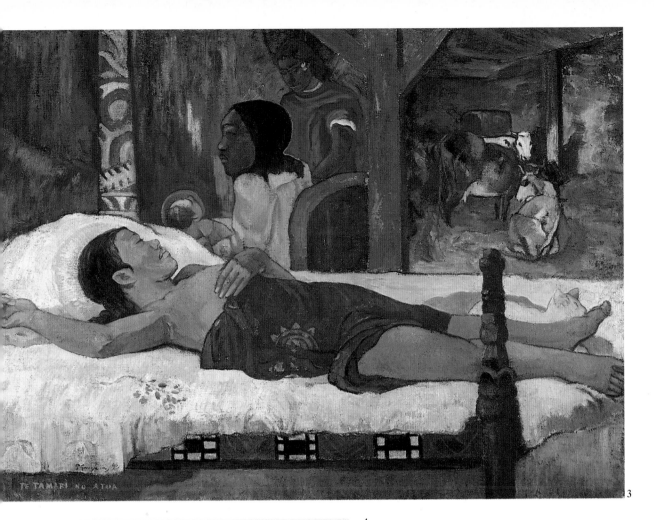

3

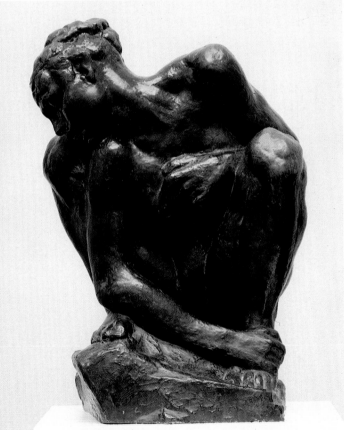

4
Auguste Rodin
Paris 1840–1917 Meudon
Crouching woman, 1880–82, signed
Bronze, 85 cm high
Inv. no. B.58. Given anonymously in
1912 as part of the Tschudi donation.
Several smaller versions in terracotta
and bronze preceded this sculpture,
for which Rodin used his model Adèle.
In the smaller versions the *Crouching
woman* is sometimes accompanied by a
male figure. The pair was made into a
group in 1882 entitled *Je suis belle*.
Rodin also intended to adapt the
larger-scale *Crouching woman* as a
caryatid.

4

Social realism and *plein-air* painting

This section features work by Dutch and German artists, among whom some men – Max Liebermann, Fritz von Uhde and Max Slevogt – were on the threshold of Impressionism. A key role was played by Liebermann, who, like his contemporary Van Gogh and other Dutch artists, was committed to nature as the basis for art, and looked for guidance to seventeenth-century Dutch painting and the Barbizon School. For these consciously middle-class artists the unadorned, citizen's art of Rembrandt, Frans Hals and the like was the model – devoted as they were to the portrayal of the simple folk, for the most part the peasantry, although later their interest extended to the urban bourgeois and eventually the industrial working classes as well.

For the Germans, Millet and Jozef Israëls were the immediate predecessors, but Liebermann, while he greatly appreciated their work, did not follow its religious symbolism. Uhde in a wide range of works gave modern form to the Christian message, and Slevogt, a kindred spirit to writers such as Gerhart Hauptmann, made unequivocal appeal to the spectator's social conscience in works such as his *Evening off* in the Gallery. However, in Liebermann's *Woman with goats among dunes* in the Gallery, one of his masterpieces, it is difficult to find any social comment.

The Dutch artists represented in this section belonged to the so-called School of The Hague, a loosely connected group who, from about 1870 in The Hague and later elsewhere as well, stressed freshness and immediacy in their painting of nature. The 'School' spans two generations, of painters born about 1830 such as Johannes Bosboom, Willem Roelofs, Jozef Israëls and Jan Hendrik Weissenbruch, and of others born about 1840, including Paul Joseph Gabriel, the Maris brothers, Anton Mauve, Hendrik Willem Mesdag and Bilders, Blommels and Neuhuys. These painters were a formative influence on Van Gogh, and were themselves formed by the native tradition of landscape painting and the work of the Barbizon School.

Max Liebermann is in many ways a complex and pivotal figure. His *Munich beer-garden* in the Gallery was directly inspired by a similar picture by Menzel, and is clearly also dependant on the Dutch realist tradition, but at the same time it reveals the influence of French Impressionism – particularly Edouard Manet's 1862 *Music in the Tuileries Gardens*. Uniting several trends, it is something of a landmark.

Max Liebermann
Berlin 1847 – 1935 Berlin
A beer garden in Munich, 1883-84, signed
Panel, 94.5 × 68.5 cm
Inv. no. 14979. Acquired in 1986 wit the aid of the Ernest von Siemens art fund.
This painting was inspired by impres sions of the Augustiner beer garden i Munich. Liebermann made numerou preparatory studies.

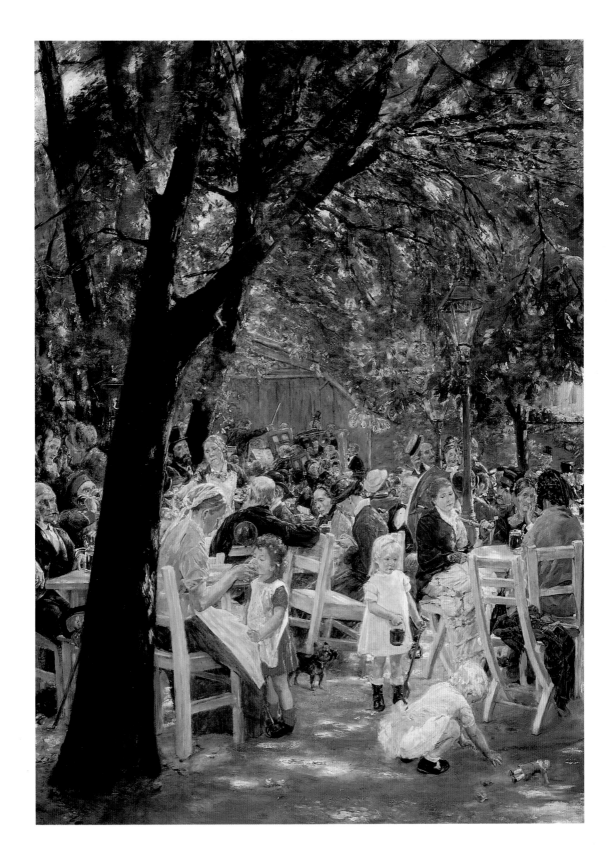

1

Max Slevogt
Landshut 1868 – 1932 Neukastel
After work, 1900-01, signed
Canvas, 126 × 155 cm
Inv. no. 8181. Acquired in 1901 at the
international art exhibition in the
Glaspalast, Munich.

Slevogt wrote of this picture: '. . . And
so I paint a couple, sitting together.
Whilst it is primarily an exercise in
painting, it should also give free rein to
darker emotions. Her face is secretive,
inscrutable. His is turned towards her.
If one needs a meaning, it will be
something like this: even the poorest
people have a right to a place at the
table of life.'

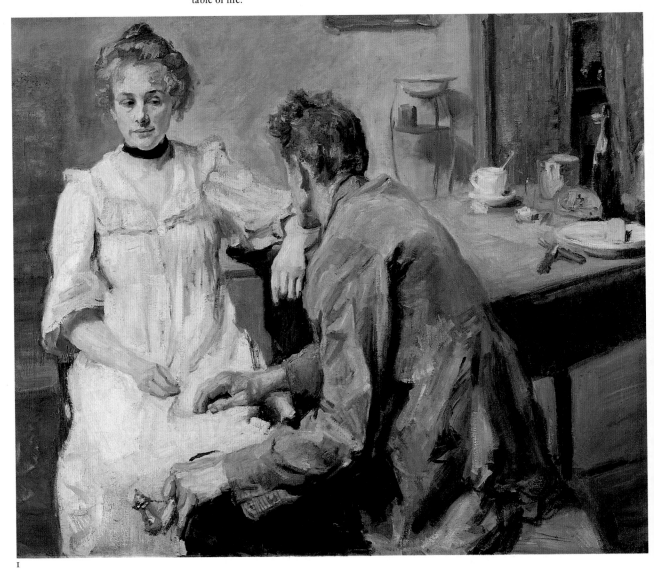

I

2
Max Liebermann
Berlin 1847 – 1935 Berlin
A woman with goats among the dunes,
1890, signed and dated
Canvas, 127 × 172 cm
Inv. no. 7815. Acquired from the artist
in 1891

3
Fritz von Uhde
Wolkenburg 1848 – 1911 Munich
The Hard Way (*The Way to
Bethlehem*), c1890, signed
Canvas, 117 × 126 cm
Inv. no. 9827. In 1890 in the collection
of Prince Regent Luitpold; acquired in
1932.
This picture is characteristic of Uhde's
method of bringing a religious subject
up to date by using contemporary
figures in biblical stories.

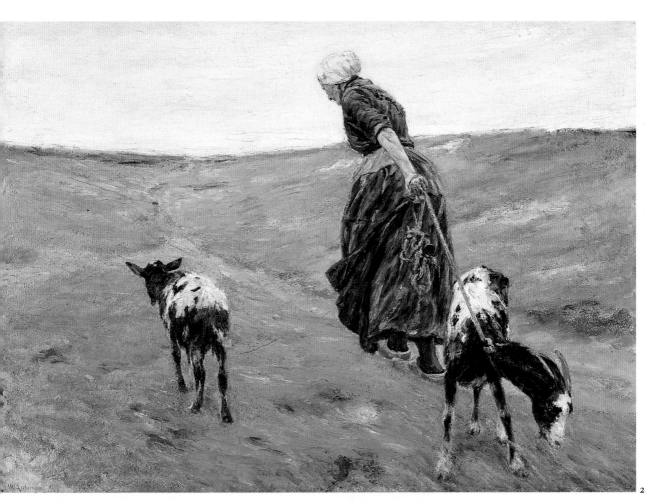

2

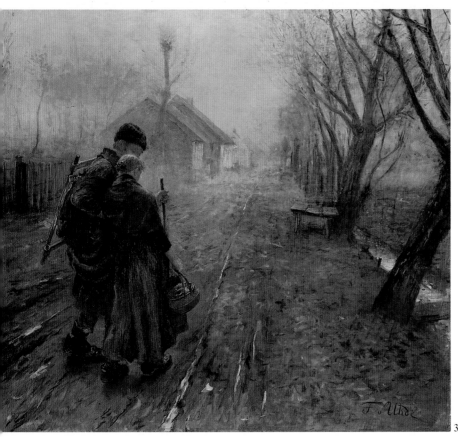

3

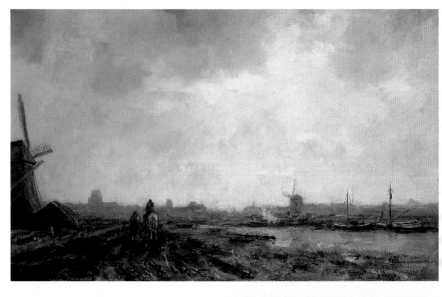

1
Jacob Maris
The Hague 1837 – 1899 Karlsbad
Dutch Landscape, 1890–91, signed
Canvas, 85 × 134 cm
Inv. no. 7838. Acquired in 1891 at the
annual exhibition in the Glaspalast,
Munich.
This work is the first of a group of oil
and watercolour landscapes in which
the artist painted variations on the
motif of a towpath.

2
Anton Mauve
Zaandam 1838 – 1888 Arnheim
Cows at the brook, late 1870s, signed
Canvas, 65.5 × 102.3 cm
Inv. no. 7766. Acquired in 1888 at the
third international art exhibition in the
Glaspalast, Munich

3
Albert Neuhuys
Utrecht 1844 – 1914 Locarno
Spring, 1885(?), signed
Canvas, 38 × 50 cm
Inv. no. 7787. Purchased by the State
in 1889

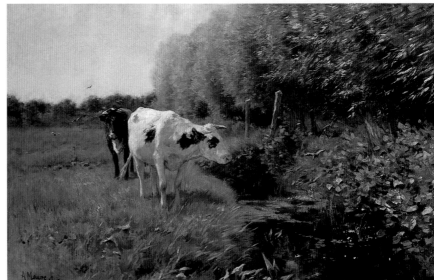

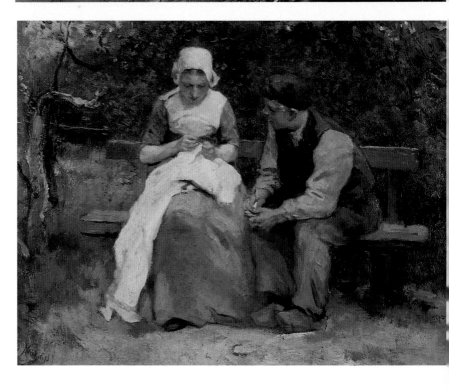

German Impressionism

Lovis Corinth
Tapiau 1858–1925 Zandvoort
The fishermen's cemetery at Nidden,
1893, signed and dated
Canvas, 113 × 148 cm
Inv. no. 12043. Acquired in 1954 from
the collection of Carl Nicolai.
Nidden was an East Prussian fishing
village and bathing resort on the
Kurische Nehrung, which came under
Soviet control in 1945.

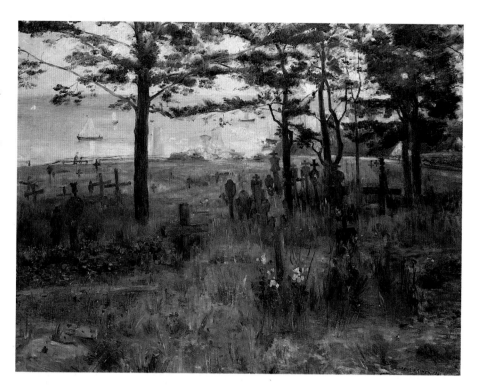

The term 'Impressionists' says even less about the German artists it is used to designate than it does about the French, but it has become widely accepted. It stands for brightly coloured, cheerful pictures, in which surface patterns have prevailed over traditional composition in terms of space and three-dimensional form. German artists, however, seldom achieved the French brilliance of colour, because they were unwilling to abandon middle tones of brown, ochre and grey. They were influenced less by early Impressionism than by the work of Van Gogh and later the Fauves, with their energetic brush-strokes and glaring, violent colours. At the same time the German artists had a greater tendency towards narrative elements and generally appealed as much to the heart and mind as the eye. In Germany, artists such as Lovis Corinth or Max Slevogt did not abandon mythological and literary subjects for the French Impressionists' almost exclusive concentration on genre, still life and landscape.

Max Liebermann, born in 1847, and Lovis Corinth and Max Slevogt, born respectively ten and 20 years later, are the three main artists of German Impressionism. In their search for rapport with nature all were inspired by seventeenth-century Dutch painting, the Barbizon School and finally also the French Impressionists, although Liebermann was a mediating influence on the other two. All three painted mostly portraits and landscapes, but Corinth was also drawn to mythological, biblical and historical subjects, and Slevogt to illustration and stage design (for productions of Goethe's *Faust* and Mozart's *Don Giovanni* and *Magic Flute*), while Liebermann increasingly turned his back on the narrative pictures of his earlier career. So, Impressionists though they may all be, the three men, more or less closely associated with other artists of some worth, such as Fritz von Uhde, were very different, too. To summarise, Liebermann was realist and objective, Corinth a spirited temperament not without his wistful moments, and Slevogt imaginative, decorative and anecdotal.

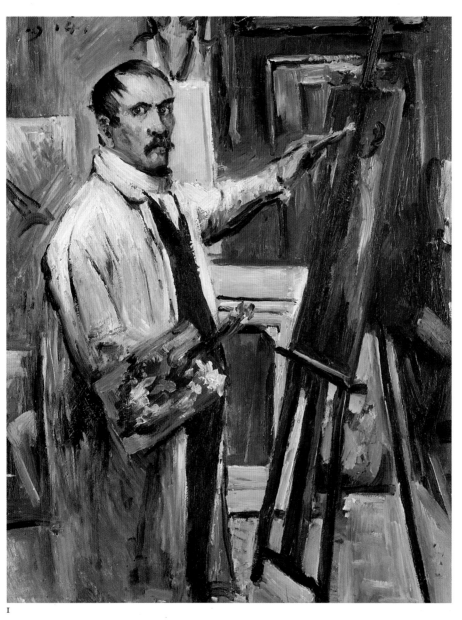

I

1
Lovis Corinth
Tapiau 1858–1925 Zandvoort
Self-portrait at the easel, 1914, signed
and dated
Panel, 73 × 57.5 cm
Inv. no. 1189. Acquired in 1950 on the
Munich art market.
The painting shows the artist after his
stroke in 1911, as a result of which his
technique changed significantly.

2
Max Liebermann
Berlin 1847–1935 Berlin
Boys bathing, 1898, signed and dated
Canvas, 122 × 151 cm
Inv. no. 14679. Given in 1980.
Liebermann painted many versions of
this theme, and also altered this
painting many times. The picture
draws on impressions of Holland,
which the artist often visited.

3
Lovis Corinth
Tapiau 1858–1925 Zandvoort
Eduard Graf von Keyserling, 1901,
signed and dated
Canvas, 99.5 × 75.5 cm
Inv. no. 8986. Acquired in 1919 on the
Munich art market.
Keyserling (1855-1918) was a short
story writer and dramatist, who suf-
fered poor health from 1893 onwards.
He was a friend of Frank Wedekind,
Karl Kraus, Max Halbe and others.

4
Max Slevogt
Landshut 1868–Neukastel 1932
*A sunny corner of the garden at
Neukastel*, 1921, signed and dated
Canvas, 90 × 110 cm
Inv. no. 9094. Acquired from the artist
in 1922.
Slevogt purchased the Neukastel estate
in the Palatinate shortly before the
First World War. It was here that he
met his future wife.

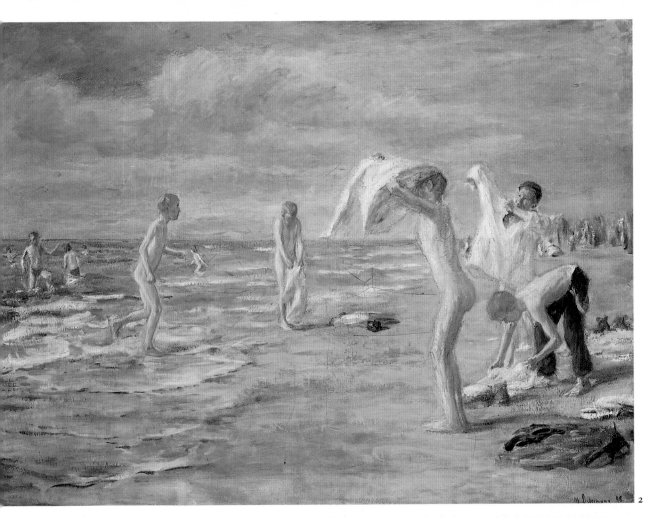

2

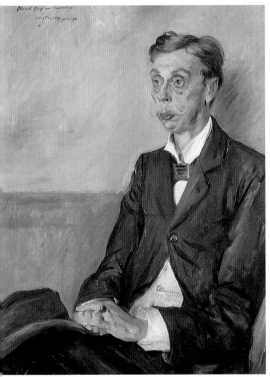

3

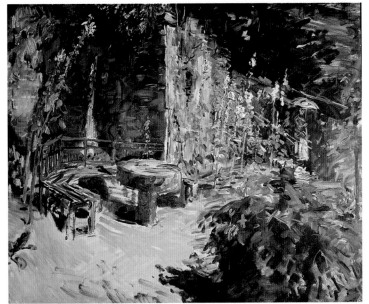

4

International art around 1900
(Symbolism, Art Nouveau)

The last section of the Neue Pinakothek illustrates various trends of the decades around the turn of the twentieth century which immediately preceded the innovations of Fauvism, Cubism and Die Brücke and Der Blaue Reiter – though some works here were made in fact after the advent of these movements. Only the two paintings by Albert Weisgerber reveal the influence of an artist such as Matisse.

In the French 'school', paintings by Claude Monet and Paul Signac exemplify the later phase of Impressionism and so-called Neo-Impressionism. In works by the Nabis or 'Prophets' (Maurice Denis, Pierre Bonnard and Edouard Vuillard) the influence of Gauguin is paramount – in their flat, decorative use of colour; Denis and also Odilon Redon adopted a symbolism reflecting to a varying extent their Christian belief.

Around 1900 a taste for unashamedly flat, highly decorative paintings was prevalent all over Europe, as an element of the style known in Germany as *Jugendstil*, in France and in the English-speaking world as *Art Nouveau*. This taste can be traced ultimately to the influence of Japanese art as it became known in the West from about 1860, and it prepared the way for the emergence eventually of abstract art. The leading centres of Art Nouveau (embracing all the arts, not least architecture) were London, Glasgow, Paris, Brussels, Munich and Vienna. Generally speaking, its most serious practitioners attempted to combine truth to nature with beauty of form, but with a new beauty, not beauty seen in terms of an historicist style.

Some artists, for instance Gustav Klimt in Vienna, transmuted their forms into precious, glittering decoration; others, such as Vuillard in France or Edvard Munch in Norway, into spectacular or nightmarish shapes. To a greater or lesser degree these artists wished to express concepts of overwhelming importance, which they did not, alas, always succeed in putting across without descent into bathos or banality. Some artists handled the grand themes of love, death and religion no more than casually, or as a means to little more than erotic titillation – the classic example is Franz von Stuck's *Sin*. Artists such as James Ensor, Egon Schiele and in particular Edvard Munch had more serious motivations, each different: Munch's imagery, combining the approach of Van Gogh and Gauguin with Nordic motifs, is genuinely affecting, and successfully conveys an impression of sinister and painful psychic forces from which there is no escape.

This was also one of Max Beckmann's major themes. In his *Crucifixion* of 1909, for which he was indebted not only to the Old Masters but also to Lovis Corinth, he used traditional subject matter, but its meaning was transformed: this is now an erotic drama of which the protagonists are a godlike hero and a 'Scarlet Woman'. Beckmann abandoned such Christian subject matter about 1920, and with the figures of the personal mythology he subsequently evolved proved to be one of the most important artists of the twentieth century.

Max Beckmann
Leipzig 1884–1950 New York
The Crucifixion, 1909, signed and dated
Canvas, 150 × 150 cm
Inv. no. L.2101. On loan from the collection of Georg Schäfer, Schweinfurt.
This painting is a major work of the artist's early period, when Beckmann was influenced not only by the Old Masters (Rubens, Rembrandt, Michelangelo) but also by more modern artists (Lovis Corinth). He transformed the symbolism of his traditional theme: the erotic relationship between a man and a woman now becomes more important than the death of the Redeemer.

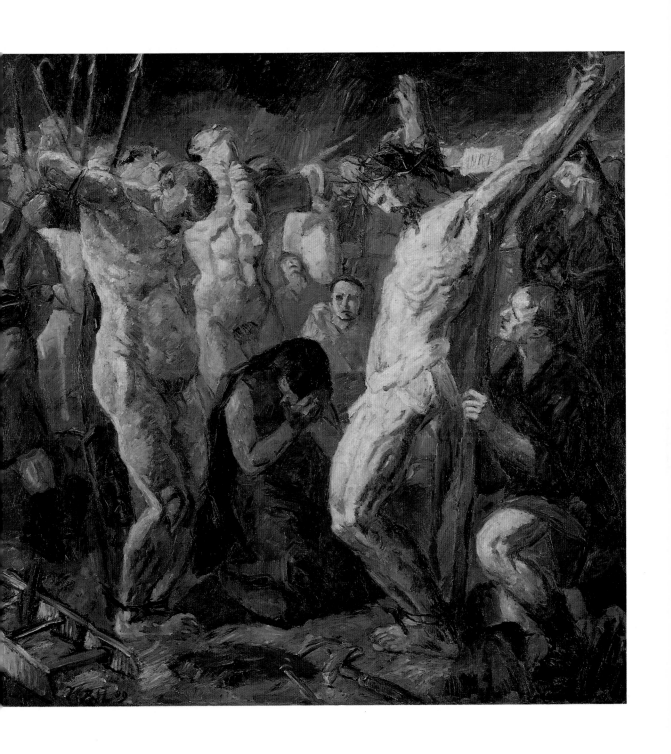

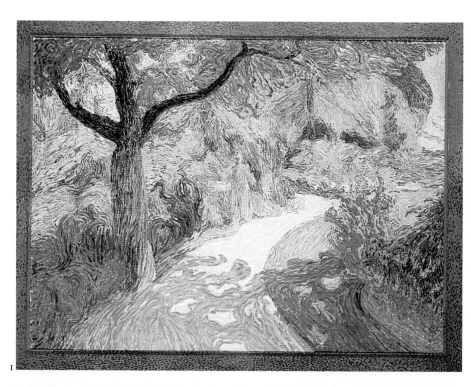

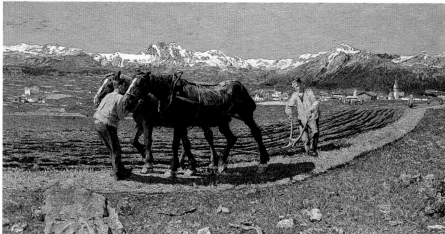

1

Henry van de Velde
Antwerp 1863 – 1957 Zurich
A garden in Kalmthout, c1892
Canvas, 70 × 95.5 cm
Inv. no. 12988. Acquired from the
estate of the artist in 1959.
Around 1890-93, the artist often used
to stay at the Villa Vogelenzang, the
house his brother-in-law and sister
occupied in Kalmthout, where he pro
duced this picture.

2

Giovanni Segantini
Arco 1858 – 1899 Pontresina
Ploughing, 1887-90, signed and dated
Canvas, 116 × 227 cm
Inv. no. 7997. Acquired in 1892 at the
exhibition of the Munich Sezession.
This picture originally existed in a
different version, which Segantini
reworked.

3

Claude Monet
Paris 1840 – 1926 Giverny
*Nympheas, c*1915, marked with the
executor's stamp
Canvas, 140 × 185 cm
Inv. no. 14562. Acquired on the
London art market in 1978.
This depicts part of the water-lily
pond which Monet had incorporated
into his estate at Giverny, and which,
in 1902, he decided to rebuild. Monet
planned his water-lily pictures as
large-scale decorative ensembles. By
1897-98, he was already making preparatory studies for them. In 1914,
when they received Georges Clemen-
ceau's backing, these projects acquired
a new urgency for Monet. Over the
following years, he produced many
pictures similar to the one in Munich.

4

Paul Signac
Paris 1863 – 1935 Paris
*On the Seine, c*1900, signed
One of four studies, oil on board, each
27 × 34 cm
Inv. no. 8658-8661. Given in 1912 by
Eduard Arnold and Robert von
Mendelssohn as part of the Tschudi
donation.
This is one of four such studies in the
Neue Pinakothek depicting the Seine
near Samois, south of Paris. Apart
from minor variations, each of the four
shows an almost identical scene though
at different times of the day.

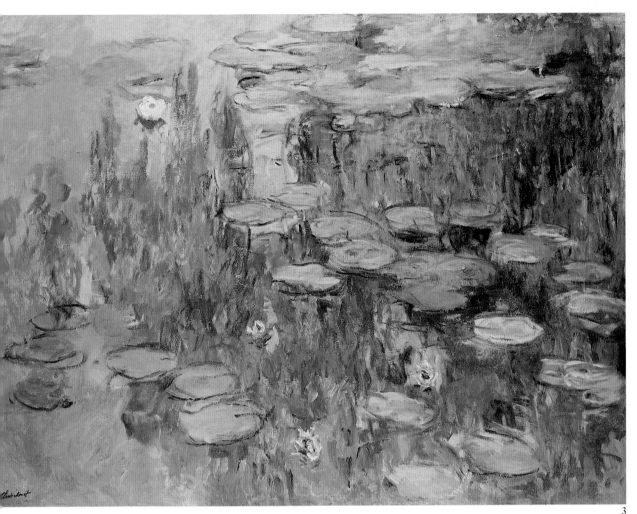

3

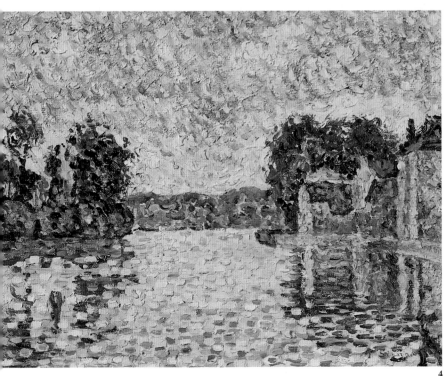

4

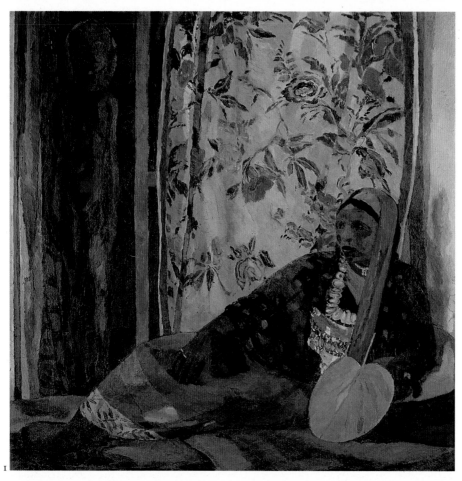

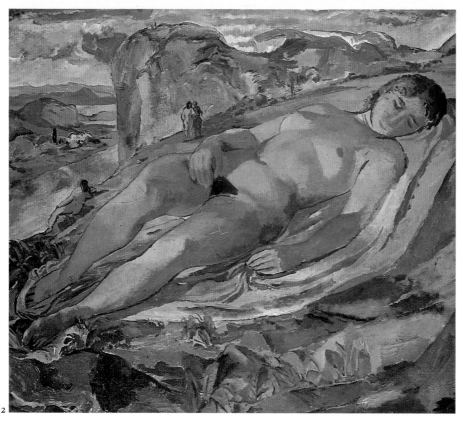

1
Albert Weisgerber
St Ingbert 1878–1915 Fromelles
A Somali woman, 1912, signed and dated
Canvas, 134 × 131 cm
Inv. no. 8693. Acquired from the artist in 1912.
This painting is based on a study of 1907 that Weisgerber had made in Hamburg.

2
Albert Weisgerber
St Ingbert 1878–1915 Fromelles
A woman lying in a hilly landscape, 1914
Canvas, 121 × 136 cm
Inv. no. 8885. Given in 1916 by Elisabeth Hesselberger.
This reclining figure is related to Weisgerber's series of pictures of Amazons. After the artist's death it was incorrectly entitled 'Mother Earth'.

3
Pierre Bonnard
Fontenay-aux-Roses 1867–1947 Le Cannet
The lignite mine in Terrenoire, c1916, signed
Canvas, 242 × 337 cm
Inv. no. 13721. Acquired from Frédéric Bonnard in 1966.
Thadée Natanson, who wrote essays on Bonnard's art, and, besides his other concerns, probably ran the lignite mine depicted here, commissioned this picture, which was evidently intended from the outset as a large-scale wall decoration.

4
Edouard Vuillard
Cuiseaux 1868–1940 La Baule
In the café, c1903, signed
Paper, 120 × 107 cm
Inv. no. 13072. Acquired in 1960 on the art market in Switzerland

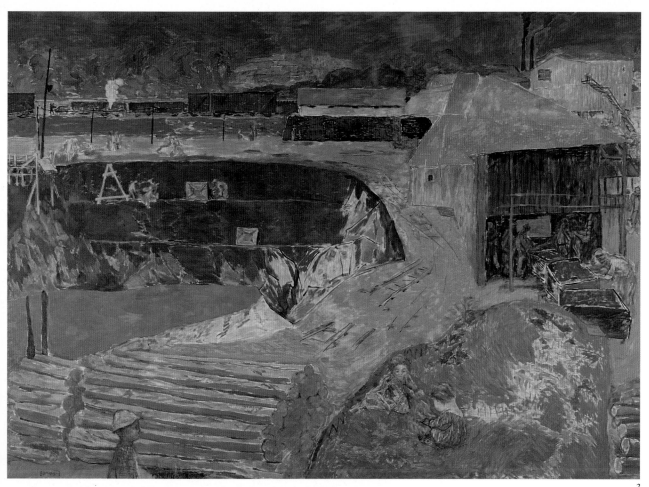

3

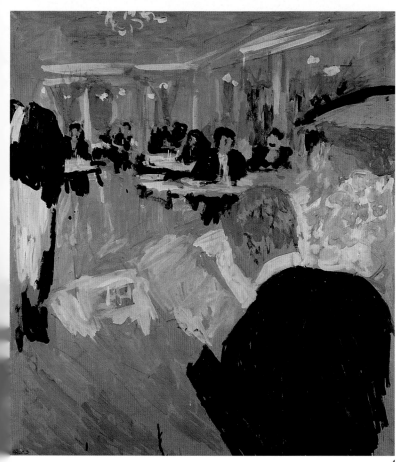

4

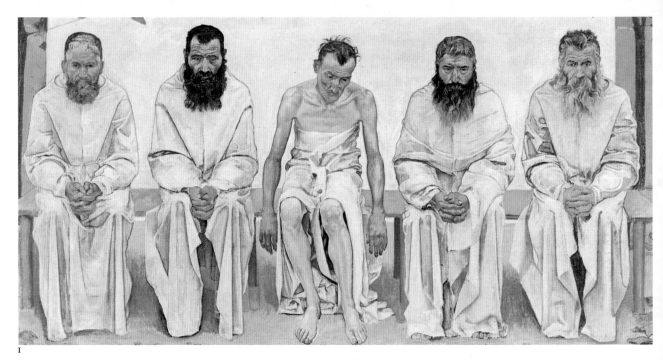

1

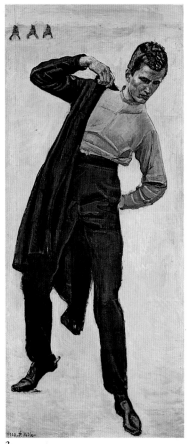

2

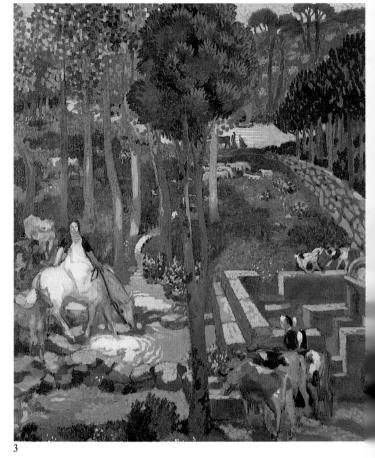

3

rdinand Hodler
rn 1853 – 1918 Geneva
red of life, 1892, signed and dated
nvas, 150 × 295 cm
v. no. 9446. Acquired in 1927 on the
unich art market

rdinand Hodler
rn 1853 – 1918 Geneva
udent of Jena in 1813, 1908, signed
d dated
nvas, 212 × 92 cm
v. no. 8643. Acquired in 1912 from
ofessor Freiherr von Bissing as part
the Tschudi donation.

is was a full-scale study for part of
odler's fresco, *The March of the Jena
dents in 1813 in the struggle for free-
m against Napoleon*, which he under-
k for Jena University.

aurice Denis
anville 1870 – 1943 Paris
ltic goddess (Epona), c1905, signed
ard, 80 × 68 cm
v. no. 8654. Given in 1912 by
uard Arnhold and Robert von
endelssohn as part of the Tschudi
nation.

ona was the Celtic goddess of horses
d other beasts of burden.

dilon Redon
rdeaux 1840 – 1916 Paris
e stained-glass window, c1912, signed
nvas, 92.5 × 73.5 cm
v. no. 13080. Acquired in 1960 from
rivate collection in Switzerland

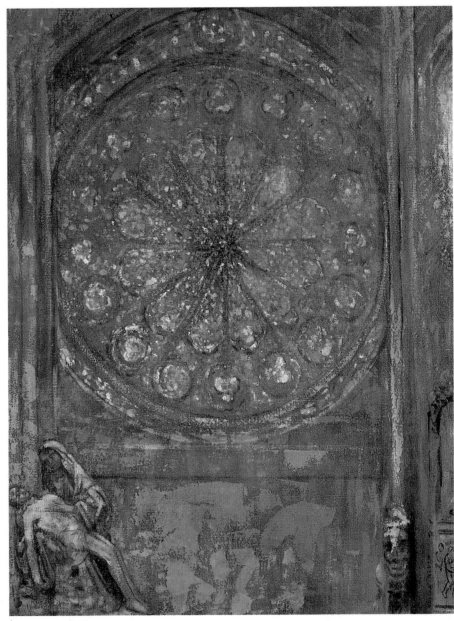

4

Fernand Khnopff
Schloss Grembergen 1858–
1921 Brussels
I lock my door upon myself, 1891,
signed and dated
Canvas, 72 × 140 cm
Inv. no. 7921. Acquired from the artist
in 1893.

The title and subject of the picture are
taken from the seventh line of the
poem *Who shall Deliver Me?*, written
in 1864 by Christina Georgina Rossetti, sister of the Pre-Raphaelite
painter. During 1891, Khnopff had
met the Pre-Raphaelite painters in
England.

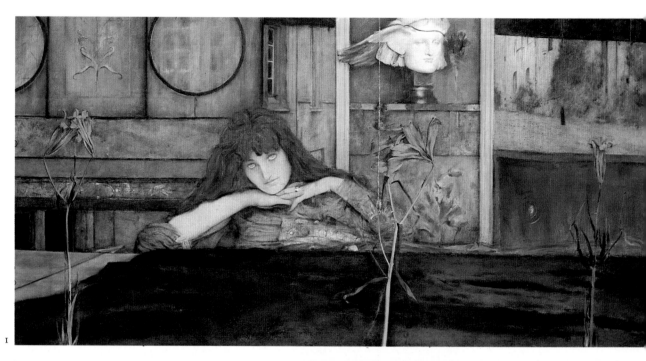

1

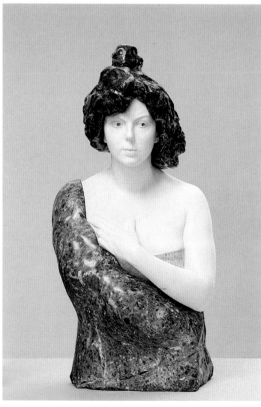

2

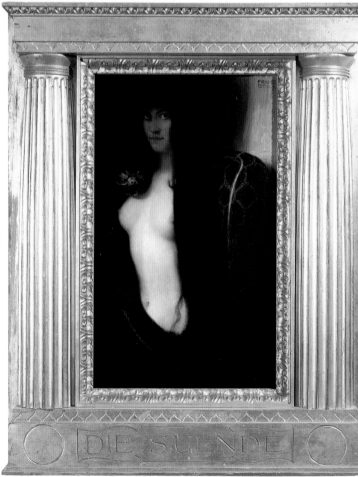

3

ax Klinger
eipzig 1857 – 1920 Grossjena
sa Asenijeff, c1900
rian marble with traces of colour
(in), inset opals (eyes), Pyrenean
arble (hair), polychrome marble of
nknown origin (drapery), 92 cm high
v. no. B.739. Given in 1981.
he writer Elsa Asenijeff, née Packeny
868-1941), came from an upper
iddle-class Austrian family and was
reviously married to a Bulgarian dip-
mat. In 1898, she met Max Klinger.
he became his model and life com-
nion, as well as the mother of his
ughter, Desirée, until they went
eir separate ways after nearly 20
ars. Elsa Asenijeff played an impor-
nt part in the Women's Movement
Diary of an Emancipated Woman,
01), led an exuberant, independent
e (trips by motorcar and motorboats,
c), and wrote about Klinger's art.
he use of a variety of sorts of marble
r the sculpture was an idea Klinger
erived from ancient Roman statuary.

ranz von Stuck
ettenweis 1863 – 1928 Munich
in, 1893, signed
anvas, 88.4 × 53 cm
v. no. 7925. Given in 1895 by
. J. Haniel.
etween 1891 and 1912, Stuck painted
any versions of this picture, in
sponse to its success with the public.

dvard Munch
ngelhaugen (in Løten) 1863 –
944 Ekely
illage street in Aasgardstrand, 1902,
gned
anvas, 59.8 × 75.8 cm
v. no. 11709. Acquired in 1953 from
he Abels Gallery, Cologne.
n 1897, in Aasgardstrand, which he
ad already visited more than once,
Munch bought a house, where he
pent some time practically every year.
Ie was there in summer 1902, when
e made his dramatic break with Tulla
arsen, whom, after a love affair last-
g four years, he refused to marry.

ames Ensor
)stend 1860 – 1949 Ostend
till life in the studio, 1889, signed and
ated
anvas, 83 × 113 cm
v. no. 13071. Acquired in 1960 from
private collection

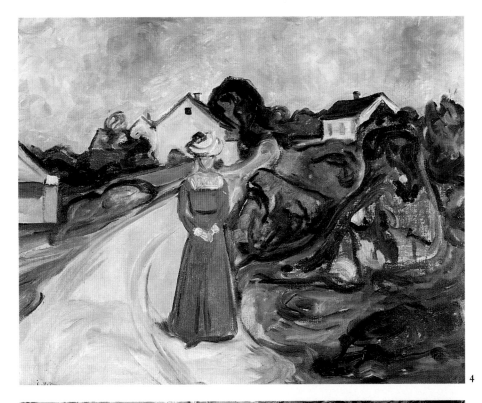

4

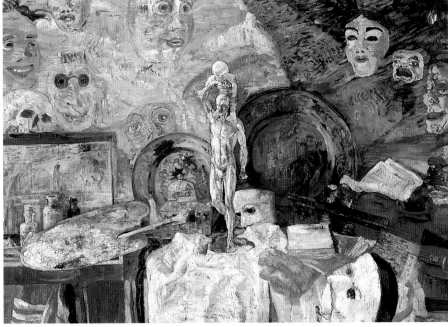

5

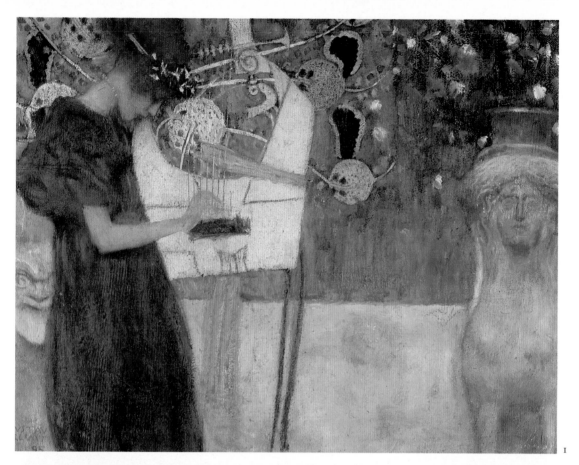

I

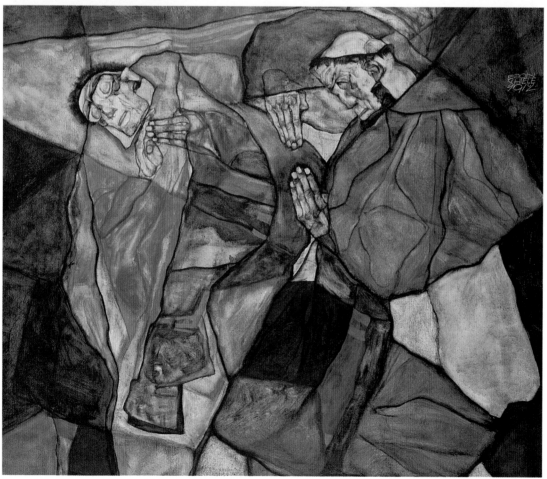

2

Gustav Klimt
Baumgarten (Vienna) 1862 –
1918 Vienna
Music, 1895, signed and dated
Canvas, 37 × 44.5 cm
Inv. no. 8195. Acquired in 1901 at the
eighth international art exhibition in
the Glaspalast, Munich.
This work was inspired by Greek vase-
painting. Klimt used the cithara and
the vine-branches to represent two
major aspects – the Apollonian and
the Dionysian – which are united here
in this allegory of music. The smaller
picture may have been a sketch for a
second, larger version, which served as
an overdoor for the music room in the
house of the Viennese industrialist
Dumba. This was destroyed in 1945.

Egon Schiele
Tulln an der Donau 1890 –
1918 Vienna
Agony, 1912, signed and dated
Canvas, 70 × 80 cm
Inv. no. 13073.
Acquired in 1960 from a private
collection in Vienna.
Depicting a dying young monk being
blessed by an older member of the
Order, this picture is a cryptic double-
portrait of Schiele as the younger
monk and of Gustav Klimt, his former
teacher, as the elder.

Gustav Klimt
Baumgarten (Vienna) 1862 –
1918 Vienna
Margarethe Stonborough-Wittgenstein,
1905, signed and dated
Canvas, 180 × 90.5 cm
Inv. no. 13074.
Acquired in 1960 from the collection
of Thomas Stonborough.
Margarethe (1882-1958) was the sister
of the pianist Paul Wittgenstein and
the philosopher Ludwig. The year this
oil was painted she married Jérôme
Stonborough.

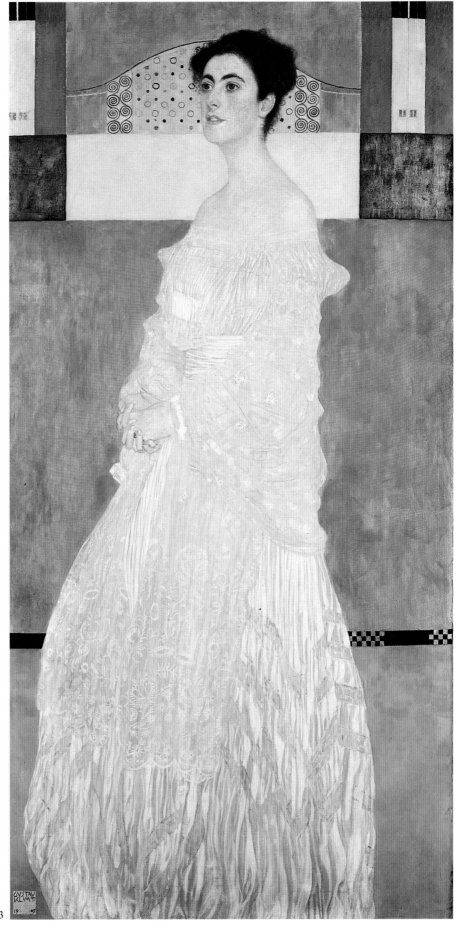

3

Bibliography

Verzeichnis der Gemälde in der Neuen Königl. Pinakothek zu München, Munich 1855

Katalog der Gemäldesammlung der Königl. Neuen Pinakothek in München, Munich 1900

Katalog der Königlichen Neuen Pinakothek zu München. 15. Auflage, Munich 1914

Katalog der Neuen Pinakothek zu München, Munich 1920

Katalog der Neuen Pinakothek zu München, Munich 1922

Gemälde Neuerer Meister aus der Neuen Pinakothek und Neuen Staatsgalerie zu München, Munich 1948

Kurt Martin, *Die Tschudi-Spende*, Munich 1962

Französische Meister des 19. Jahrhunderts. Ausgestellte Werke I, Neue Pinakothek und Staatsgalerie, Munich 1966

Meisterwerke der deutschen Malerei des 19. Jahrhunderts. Ausgestellte Werke II, Neue Pinakothek und Staatsgalerie, Munich 1967

Malerei der Gründerzeit (= *Bayerische Staatsgemäldesammlungen Neue Pinakothek/München, Gemäldekataloge VI*), bearbeitet von Horst Ludwig, Munich 1977

Nach-Barock und Klassizismus (= *Bayerische Staatsgemäldesammlungen, Neue Pinakothek/München, Gemäldekataloge III*), bearbeitet von Barbara Hardtwig, Munich 1978

Neue Pinakothek. Erläuterungen zu den ausgestellten Werken, Munich 1981

Erich Steingräber, *Die Neue Pinakothek München*, Munich 1981

Festgabe zur Eröffnung der Neuen Pinakothek in München am 28. März 1981, Munich 1981

Museum: Neue Pinakothek München, Brunswick 1981

Christoph Heilmann, *Neue Pinakothek München*, Munich and Zurich 1984

Spätromantik und Realismus (= *Bayerische Staatsgemäldesammlungen Neue Pinakothek/München, Gemäldekataloge V*), bearbeitet von Barbara Eschenburg, Munich 1984

Neue Pinakothek. Erläuterungen zu den ausgestellten Werken. 5. Auflage, Munich 1988

Index